T0062846

OLD THOUGHTS
FOR A MODERN AGE

More Poems from an Autistic Poet,
Now with multiple sclerosis

Joy Olree

abbott press

Abbott Press books may be ordered through booksellers or by contacting:

Abbott Press
1663 Liberty Drive
Bloomington, IN 47403
www.abbottpress.com
Phone: 1-866-697-5310

ISBN: 978-1-4582-1736-3 (sc)
ISBN: 978-1-4582-1737-0 (e)

Library of Congress Control Number: 2014913571

Printed in the United States of America.

Abbott Press rev. date: 08/08/2014

This book I dedicate to my family and friends, but mostly to the residents at the Huntingdon Health and Rehabilitation nursing home. This is where I will live when my MS makes it impossible for me to care of myself.

Acknowledgements: The cover art painted by Joy Olree. It is acrylics, painted with toothpicks

MY NEW BOOK

My new book, yes I'm back. Still an undiagnosed autistic, but now I have MS. A lot has happened since my first book" Coffee Cup Stains Thoughts From an Austic Poet" I now have my own website and I blog. Blogging allows me to say what I want uncensored, but I try to never say or write anything that would be censored, my thoughts are another story, they run wild on occasion. Blogging is great except for the comment spam. Comment spam is spam masked as a comment. In my second blog post I said I wondered if anybody was reading my posts. The next day I had 1,ooo what I thought was comments to my blog post. I thought wow 1,000 folks read my post and commented. I was on cloud 9, I did a little bragging the next day. Then the 1,000 increased to 2,000, then 3, 000, then 5,000, my internet provider was not amused. AOL said you do indeed have unlimited e-mail rights but a folder only holds 5,000 e-mails, if you are going to get over 5,000 e-mails start another folder. Well, being the tech idiot I am, I did not know what to do, how to start another folder. I had never even got 1,000 e-mails let alone 5,000. I bought 3 books on blogging and that's where I learned what comment spam was. By this time my comments/spam had gotten up to over 700,000. AOL was very unhappy, so was I. I deleted comments until I *thought my hand was going to die. It started out 1,000 a Day then quickly went up to 10,000 a day so I called AOL to see what they could do or what advice they could give me to do. The lady I spoke to said," When did you start having this problem, "I said, "when I started blogging." She said" blogging you have a blog, "I said yes. Then she said, "Well those comments are people who want to talk to you, you should not delete them, and she laughed." I said," Mam this morning I had 12,000 comments. There is no way possible I could respond to that many people* even if I wanted to and I don't want to.. She said, "Ok I'll take your e-mail address off the blog so they can't mail you, but you need to call your website host to get them to block the comment spam." I called them and they laughed too, well I was not laughing, but they fixed the problem. I still; blog when my MS will allow but I still have many unanswered comments on my blog. Some of them are Spam but some are not and the whole process is time and energy consuming, which I have little of. I have gotten my comments down from 700,000 to 10,000, so that is a big improvement. I am sure I deleted comments from people who truly wanted to talk to me but I did not do it on purpose and I will do better in the future. Even though I have MS I still paint and of course write.

Most of my family has died, my father I believe had died when the first book came out, now my step-mom has died and my dad's sister and brother and 1 uncle. I now have 3 blood aunts left and 2 aunts and 1 uncle by marriage left, 3 kids and 8 grandchildren. One husband, yes he's still here too, soon we will have been together 22 years. Wow who would have ever believed it possible? If looking at other women was a disease, he would have been dead years ago. Once he even chased one, so to speak, but he never caught her never even spoke to her, it was a mental thing you know, but he's still mine.

Since my last book I have been diagnosed with MS, thank God now I finally know what has been wrong with me since I was 10 years old. Most people with MS, at least those with it years ago were not able to get an accurate diagnosis because MS is hard to diagnose, at least until now. Now there are better means of detecting MS so people today don't go through everything I had to. To tell you of all the X-rays and various MRIS, blood tests and other things I had to go through would be another book, but I will say, it took a ride in an ambulance to the ER 3 years ago to find out I have MS. In the recent 10 years or so there have been many treatments and medicines developed for MS so I now have things I can take and do for my MS. They say MS won't kill you but the side effects of the medicines and complications from the MS can. But I am not willing to throw my hands up in the air yet. One thing that always gives me a chuckle is one of the newer medicines says one of the side effects is death so be sure to call your doctor if you experience this. Ok but how would one do this after death?

My husband is not what you would call caregiver, but he does his best and thank goodness I have him. The children are not caregivers either. Actually I and God handle my MS needs. In truth MS is a very strange unpredictable disease. I just barely understand it so how I could expect anyone else to. I knew my son did not understand MS when his wife said there would never be a handicap ramp at their house for me because it looked tacky and I hardly ever came there anyway. Maybe if they had a ramp I would come more, I mean I am in a wheel chair part of the time. My other children live in other states. The thing that gets me is my children say oh mom you will never have to go to a nursing home because we will take care of you. Really when it that going to happen? Well it's my MS and I intend to keep moving as long as I can by whatever means I can. If no one else wants to help me and I get to the point I can't do for myself I am going to a nursing home which is fine by me.

At present I give myself 3 injections a week to slow down the progress of my MS and I take a pill to help with my walking. I also take eye vitamins because MS is affecting my eyesight and potassium because I drink so much tea that it depletes my potassium. Once I had to go to the ER in an ambulance because of this. My doctor said, give up the tea or take a potassium tablet. "I said, "I was born allergic to milk so I started drinking tea when I was 1 year old, give me the potassium tablets the tea stays."

I would tell you that my heart is broken because of the deaths in my family but that would be a lie and I don't lie. Death happens to us all one day, when, only God knows but it will happen. Ever know anybody that did not die? Well there, point proved. My parents spent their last days in a nursing home and although my dad hated being away from his home he would not leave my step-mom, who had to be there.

I still go to church, God is my God and his son died for me, what is not clear to me is why more folks don't go to church. I mean if you don't go to church how will you worship God and if you don't worship God how can you have any hope of getting into Heaven? Of course now don't get me wrong Gods church is not the building it is the members but you have to admit having a building to worship in makes it easier to worship God and the Bible clearly says there has to be at least 2 people worshiping together for God and Christ to be there.

Now if you don't want to worship God it's your choice/freewill you know. But there is that Hell thing. If you are not living your life in a way that is pleasing to God, well on

Judgment Day he has said he will send you there forever. Scary right, at least for me so I read my Bible, pray and go to church 3 times a week. Will that get me into Heaven I sure hope so, but I will find out on Judgment Day. There is a song on the radio by Lorde and she sings that she is not ready to throw her hands up in the air, well neither am I.

There has been a lot of debate as to whether or not we will know anybody in Heaven, now as for me I don't care one way or the other as long as I get there. I hate the thought of people I care about going to Hell, but if that is what they decide I am not going with them if I can help it. Ok as for my preaching, I think I'm done, for the moment.

I visit a nursing home every day. It is the same nursing home my parents were in. See I got in the habit of visiting them there and I made many friends there and I love them and they love me. Sadly some of them die and I grieve but I am so glad I was their friend. I have seen so much physical problems there it makes my MS seem like nothing.

I have a new grandchild Audrey and she is walking now, her parents live in Georgia, their names are Virginia and Sausan Lak. She is a school teacher and he is a soccer coach. They met here in Mckenzie at Bethel University, where they were married and almost killed by me, ever hear of a Bridezilla, well my sweet precious daughter became one. She at one point threatened a court house marriage if she did not get the wedding she wanted, I said fine it will save me some money. Virginia was the child that wrote 2 of the poems in my first book Coffee Cup Stains, Thoughts From An Autistic Poet. In case you were wondering the wedding cost me 7,000.

My middle daughter and her husband live in Kentucky and in my first book she was called the wild child, but she is not wild anymore. My son lays brick, he and his wife have 3 children and live in Mckenzie where I live.

All in all my life is still the same I just have MS, which I have had since I was 10 but I never knew it, I just thought I was strange.

Buy my book don't buy it I have said what I wanted to say and I paid to say it so there. It's not so bad being an autistic poet with MS, because I still have God and he still has me.

What my future holds for me I don't know but I have a grandchild married now so I expect great grandchildren one day. One day at the time, one moment at a time is what I have and I and God can handle that. Bye for Now Joy Olree the Autistic poet now with MS. And I am on Twitter and Face book too, so come follow me I love all of you.

13 ROSES

13 roses' broken hearts
30 silver coins. 9 lives,
12 apostles, 1 Jesus,
1 God. 2 thieves,
1 repented, 1 saved.
12 months, 1 year,
7 days. 1 week,
4 seasons, I universe,
1 Devil.

Many things, many
numbers, birthdays,
holidays, death and
taxes.

Seems to me, 1 Jesus +
1 God + 1 Devil, means
trouble right here on
earth, unless we wake
up and smell the roses.

A CHILD

Saw a child on a corner
lost in his despair. Left
a dime in his cup, walked
away
At Heaven's gate this child
sits on a seat of judgment.
He points at me and says,
"Keep on walking no dime
for you, nothing but Hell."

A FAMILIAR TASTE OF POISON

Your lips, so red so soft, their
words seduce, their meanings
clearly meant to deceive.

Oh, if only I could resist, but
death seems a small price to
pay for a familiar taste of
poison. A poison so deadly
yet sweet, that even though
these lips are not hers, my fate
is assured.

A HOLY WAR AND ITS MUSIC

Holy shirt and underwear,
naked legs and music,
sing for your soul, plead
for understanding, wish
there was a means to stop
whatever path this is.

Late night artistic creations,
daytime refreshment sleep.
The in-between foolishness,
best meant for reflection of
what it is that's needs doing
for the salvation of the soul.

A KISS AND 40 PIECES

With a kiss and 40 pieces of silver my savior
was betrayed. Before the cock crowed 3 times
he was denied by 1 of his 12. Innocent he lived
innocent he died.

Father can this sacrifice ever be justified by a
sinner like me? Father if it had been possible
would I have taken his place?

I will never know, but I thank you for the
opportunity to meet Jesus in Heaven with a
kiss and 40 pieces of eternal gratefulness.

A LIFE WITHOUT HOPE

I can only imagine
a life without hope,
I can only pretend
it so because with
the death of Gods
son hope is what
I have.

A PRAYER

Midnights' new day, the light
still hours away. Sleep won't
come, thoughts don't stop. In
my mind I see the cross the
nails in innocent flesh.

Paradise seems so far away
sin so close. Oh God hear my
prayer, forgive this sinner. Help
me understand your will. Keep
my feet strong so I can walk with
Jesus until the day appointed for
judgment.

FOR A TASTE OF SIN

A taste of death,
a lovers quest.
Weakness of flesh,
a moments folly.
Lifetimes ridged
conduct, sacrificed
at the bequest of
beauty and sin.

A TROUBLED SOUL

A troubled soul I fear.
For how can man delight
in sin and consequence,
when an invitation is given
to share eternity with God
our father.

AUTUMN

An Autumn war
for summers end,
its' fight between
gravity and leaves.
Colors they change,
temperatures too,
all to prepare for
winters cold.

DARKEST NIGHTS

Rain pain, dark mark sail fail, run sun.
white bright light night, sleep tight feel
right.

Deep loose gay goose, send friend, drop
top, shout out, foul mouth, sin fit, dim wit.

Loud proud, stiff necked, reject defect,
detest recessed, distressed humanity.

Black sight soul fright, my plight keep quiet,
fear not life's strife, sleep sound.

Safe there, where meant, those chose. Slim
none, a sinners chance for Heavens home.

Odds favor the Devils' Hell to keep those
humans that thought they knew it all.

DAYBREAK COMES

Daybreak comes as
night drifts into sleep.
Morning flows through
land and sea.

Life stirs, actions resume,
the earth is once more
allowed to be.

Seems God is not ready
to destroy us yet

HOW DEEP IS YOUR LOVE

Hung on a cross between two thieves,
the son of God innocent and good,
vinegar for water, ridiculed and
mocked, yet with his dying breath he
cried, "father forgive them for they
know not what they do."

Love so deep, the son of God died for
a sinner me. What have I done to deserve
such sacrifice? Can I ever repay this debt
I owe?

How deep is your love? Jesus' love was
endless. He said, "come all yea that will."
How deep is your love? Would you give
your life for anyone, let alone all. How
deep is your love? Is it deep enough to
keep you out of Hell.

DIALOGUE WITH THE DEVIL

Hells doorway to a dream. I'm not real,
do not worry. Live life to the fullest,
grab all the gusto you can find.

Un oh I lied, does it hurt? I mean you
are screaming. No God won't save you
now. How long is eternity? Forever. Parole,
ha, ha.

How good was that sex, do you still want a
beer? Monkey see monkey do, no you did
not come from there. Who's your daddy?
Yeah God, remember him.

Oh well I guess I'm retired now, I mean since
the earth is gone. Why am I doing this? You
think I have a choice? Hey God don't play and
I did rebel. I guess the jokes on me and you,
misery loves company you know.

Oh shut up, you had your chance. No I don't
know where your children are, I know where you
are. God is not listening, you killed his son, deal
with it.

DEVINE REBELLION

Sacred evil, unwritten,
unremembered divine
rebellion.

Evil of heart, foolish
uprising, destined to
fail.

Simple truths God
provoked, a force
unleashed, Hell created
the Devil it's ruler.

EXCUSES

What's your excuse now?
One day, maybe tomorrow,
today not convenient.

Death wait I'm not ready,
God wait I'm not ready.
Satan got any water, help.

FALLEN

Fallen leaves and mustard seeds,
the biggest hope of tiny faith. If
only we would be as God designed
for us to be, then maybe this could
be a real nice place to live.

FALSE PREACHERS

Where he leads
we should follow,
but false words
can condemn, are
the sermons you
preach Gods words
or Satan's?

FROGS AND BEASTS

Froggie friendly kiss a prince, take a chance, do your best.
Trapped beauty, scented vex, a rose dying in a crystal vase.

For love of unknown beauty spells are broken, but who will
love a beast whose beauty is hidden in fur and feathers.
Slimy green skin, cold to touch.

Froggie, froggie, wait don't be trapped forever in this hideous
appearance. Remember is was for anger and careless actions
this was brought upon you,

A hardened heart scared of rejection, will run off every hope
for change. Look inside and find the kindness that existed
before frogs and beasts

GOOD LIFE

Live for rewards saved for the future lean on the one that cares. Stay away from temptation, see the beauty in righteousness, fear punishment for sin. Trouble seems to follow a weak soul. Strength can carry you through the lowest moments in human life.

If Jesus saves, can anything destroy but the Devil? He's not a man in a red suit with a pitch fork, but his costume is evil, his words sweet and deceptive.

You might meet him at Wal-Mart, the grocery store. Believe it or not he might even be in your church.

How can you recognize him? Read your bible, if it's not in there then it's probably the Devil.

A good life seems desirable and it could be okay but don't let life be so good that it sends you to Hell

HIGHER

Love is taking me higher I scream for joy,
I scream for love, passion and healing
Higher I soar, who knows where I stop.

If love was all that was, oh what a
wonderful world it would be. But if
love was all that was, would Jesus have
had to die for our sins? Would our sins
have been forgiven, would there have
been any sins to forgive?

But there was sin in the world and Jesus
did die for our sins. Yes love is wonderful
and while we are here on earth, it sure
makes life enjoyable until the day we meet
Jesus face to face.
Love is taking me higher and one day it will
take me to heaven

CAN I GET A LITTLE HIP HOP IN HEAVEN?

Hey God, I know I'm just a humble servant,
but I was wondering, is it possible, could
I get a little Hip Hop in Heaven?

Gospel music is great but I really love me
some Jo Lo. Now I don't know that she's
a Christian, but her music makes me happy
when I'm feeling sad.

God, can you honestly say when Dylan
sings knocking on Heavens door, it does
not make you smile just a little.

Why it would not surprise me one bit, to see
the angels in Heaven doing the moon walk.

Hey I know you're in control and I respect
that, but if it be your will could I get a little
Hip Hop in Heaven?

I AM NOT BOB DYLAN

I am not Bob Dylan or Leonard Cohen,
but there is this Buddhist monk that
lives on Mt. Baldy, I sometimes look up
on the internet, just to see if he's still alive.

He's a hundred and three, my husband
studied with him three years, he says he
has an amazing laugh.

I liked to see him in Heaven but he doesn't
believe in that, says he's looking for nirvana.
It's not a place it's a level of consciousness.

I hope he's right because if he's wrong, Hell
will kill his amazing laugh.

IF IT AIN'T BROKE DON'T FIX IT

What's wrong with usefulness?
because new and better will be
obsolete tomorrow.

Remember outhouses. Now toilets
flush themselves. First time I sat
down on one of those it scared the
shit out of me. Here I was doing my
business and the toilet flushes and
I was not done.

Well I don't know about the rest
of you but the first time one of
those tries to wipe my ass, I'm
out of there and I won't be back.

Seems we'd have learned by now
if it ain't broke don't fix it.

IMPORTANT

Important take notice,
it's over, never really
started. Can't say I'll
miss what I never had,
but it would have been
nice if for just a moment
to have seen the other
side of could have been.

JESUS CAME

Jesus came but many did not believe.
The son of God died salvations object
because some loved the praises of men
more than truth and justice.

Now judgment comes for all who reject
the son of God.

If life exist, which it must, if these words
are read, then there is still time to accept
Jesus as Gods son.

Heaven or Hell the choice is yours, A
paradise or a burning fire. Birth starts
the journey to the beginning of your eternity.
Death is the door that lets you in.

KEEP YOUR EYES ON ME

Many sights to see, beauty all around.
ugliness too and sometimes it's hard
to know the difference because the
Devil is so tricky, he's the master of
disguise he can make anything look
good until you touch it.

These eyes of mine sometimes fail to
see what is meant to be seen. God never
intended me to worship other things, so
he said, "keep your eyes on me to know
what's right, but if by chance you touch
some seemingly good thing to discover
it's not, ask for forgiveness and keep
your eyes on me."

KEYS

Keys to lock
unlocked doors,
chains to bind
unbound fools.
Staves to pierce
unmarked leaves,
a blade of grass,
a rule of law.

Remarkable though,
there seems to be,
endless beauty for
all to share,
when greed and
selfishness tear it
up.

LAST DAY

If today were your last day, what
would be said about you? Missed
chance or safety dance, fiery flames
or crystal clouds, songs of praise
or screams of pain.

Behind clouds of shadow hides
truth and lies, where will your
shadow fall?

Will life lead down a narrow path,
or run down a widen road? For many
come but few enter.

Stop thoughts of sin and pleasure,
treasure service to God in Heaven.
Fleeting time could end right now.
Will your Kodak moment be a
horror show or a paradise?

LESSONS FROM A SUNDAY MORNING SERMON

Submit remit detest a fallen man.
Request a given redemption,
salvation by decree.

For naught can be refused that
truly would receive by grace
and understanding.

A fathers' loving words, who gave
his only son, to die a horrid death
for sinners just like me.

LIFE IS FOR

Life is for living
within Gods borders.
Life is for giving as
has been prospered.
Life is for loving
as you are loved.
Life is for dying at
appointed times.
Life is for judgment
for the in-between
birth and death.

MAMMA I'M COMING HOME

16, I was, innocent and poor.
Daddy did his best but the
Devil looked good, especially
since I blamed God for taking
you from me.

Years of sin brought temporary
pleasure but no peace.

I almost let my anger at God
keep me from you, but I could
not forget what I knew was right.

So with a lot of prayer and Gods
help, mamma I'm coming home.

NEVER WAS

I am me no more.
Never was really,
anything more than
a creation of God.

A child of light
surrounded by
darkness, a weakened
spirit does naught but
make cracks for the
dark to get in.

As the hour of death
approaches will there
be hope of a Heavenly
home or fear of a home
in fire.

NOTHINGNESS

When the moon stood still
and the earth shook, the wind
refused to blow. The water
stopped its' flow and man in
all his glory was reduced to
nothingness.

ONE MOMENT

One moment of time
a lifetime of service,
blessed assurance of
Heavens' abode.

Keep worries of today
where they belong, in
God's hands.
Fear not fate for in due
time all things are done,
not by our design but by
the will of the father in
Heaven.

If it should be it will be.
Why trouble yourself,
remember the lilies of the
field, the birds of the air.
Does not God provide for
them, will he not also you.
If we believe Heaven, to be,
as is written in the Bible, why
then do we cling so fiercely to
this sinful world.

PARADISE WAITS

Paradise waits as
souls are sacrificed.
Sin is revealed, death
imminent, punishment
assured, forgiveness
the cure, asking the key.

PARADISE

Can't escape this feeling.
A love paradise, life sucks
without you.

Friends hear tears of regret,
see a future of doubt. Wait to
know fate. Present distress
seems to take away a moments
joy.

Certainty of death a constant
reminder of where I failed.

PERFECT BUT NOT OKAY

Short people want to be tall,
tall people want to be short.
The end between seems
meager fare.

Whatever happened to I'm
okay you're okay? We want to
look like Angelina or Brad,
Cher or Denzel.

Our boobs are too small, we
need a tummy tuck, face lift
and liposuction, and these
wrinkles got to go. Such
nonsense, madness, 30,000 to
please yourself, humanity,
what?

Stressing about reality while
God watches and smiles, thinking
I love you just the way you are.

PLACE

Take place in present moments,
lose memories dead and gone.
Future dreams will never come
because now is in control.

Present thoughts, lose importance
when futures are unsure. Take the
past, to learn what's best for living
in the now.

Mistakes forgotten, reappear, just
in time, to cause more problems
for human kind.

It is best, to remember fallen times
then to continue repeating past
mistakes.

A POEM OF CHILLING FALL

Water flows, flowers bloom
as silence stirs its restless
soul. Music sooths a listeners
heart as time and tragedy go
to meet a welcomed guest.

PRICE TAG

Putting price over truth,
is everything for sell?
Left right up down, it
should not be about the
money, even though it
often is.

All the bling, bling, and
the ching, ching. What
good is it, if it sends you
to Hell.

RANDOM WISDOM

Catch and carry freight for sale,
where there's sure to be some
poor soul destined to fall short.

His requirements seem so strict,
making one shudder at thoughts
of Heavens rejection and Hells
acceptance.

Beef lost to man as pigs and
people fill the earth with trash.

Soft rhythms, entice the soul,
to lead astray from what's been
taught as right.
Humble scared we needs must
be, for on our own can naught
be done.

In Gods eyes straight and tall,
must man stand, for where has it
been written that he requires any
less?

SACRED AMENITIES

Sacred amenities, cash for soul,
sounding boards, pet grievances,
nothing is acceptable, everything
is wrong.

Hate to think tomorrow might be
lost, living in the now, to serve a
risen God who died for me.

The glitter of life a wonder and
confusion, witnessing but never
sure the right of anything.

Could seemingly angels be devils
in disguise? Will 3-d be the next
false god as truth becomes obsolete.

Video whores and reality illusions
grab attentions best used for a study
of Gods' requirements.

SALVATION

Saved by Jesus,
washed in holy
blood, tempted
by the Devil and
stained by sin, but
forgiven by prayer.

SEARCHING

Searching mountain tops,
desert plains and darken
skies. Making collections
deemed necessary to ensure
prosperity of body and soul.

A risen savior watches as
tiredness descends on flesh
and bones leaving nothing
wanting except eternal rest
with God.

SHE NEVER MENTIONED GOD TO ME

Clap appreciation,
smile away misery,
a little kindness
goes a long way.

Wouldn't is be tragic
on judgment day to
hear someone say,
"she never mentioned
God to me."

SLEEP COMES FIRST

Stop being so hard on yourself,
see the means to an end of your
own making. Take careful steps
bones break, hearts too. Realize
the, wonderful creation that is
you.

Seems life shatters dreams in
favor of fear. But truth be known
fear is often nothing more than
irrational foolishness caused by
overzealous humans with no time
for God so they create drama in a
futile attempt to control life, as if
God was nonexistent.

When will we stop listening to all
this nonsense. Sure would be good
if it could be before God steps in
and shows us the error of our ways.

SOCIAL RESPONSIBILITY

Social responsibility
ignorance no excuse.
Feign regret choose
repression over
awareness, pretend
it won't happen, Hell
that is.

Imagine a world
without sin, a world
without God then wake
the f--- up and go to
church.

You may think you know
it all but one day you will
see just how little you do
know

SOUNDS OF A UNIVERSE

The whisper of a blade of grass,
the laughter of a fallen leaf. The
sigh of polluted waters, crying
clouds and screaming trees. I
pray to save the symphony, that
once was natures paradise.

Man destroys, for what he claims
is the greater good, promising to
repair, but he forgets that what is
destroyed today will take years to
replace.

At our present rate of destruction
it will all be gone before time can
rebuild it.

STYLE

Style is going my way and past.
Simple and secure decided to
stay. Careful does not seem to
suffice guaranteed doubts over
future requests.

Make the clothes that make the
man, sold the world a pack of
lies. Felt it was not wise to tell
the truth when dollars and cents
pay the way.

SUDDENLY

Suddenly
I'm feeling
very small,
one step
beyond
death as
youth
runs the
show.

SWALLOWED

Swallowed in a sea of sin,
trampled in fields of should
have done.

Caste aside by had a chance,
punished for what was done.

But saved by innocent blood
through service and obedience.

THE EDGE OF LIFE

As one soul swept away,
loves' embrace left to die.
Wings of gold washed
ashore, the blood stained
innocence.

Of slaughtered saints and
tarnished angels, a white
doves' last flight.

The edge of life its'
sharpened truth, a glorious
dancers' pointed feet, the
seasoned prophets' written
words, here but not.

THE EMPTY SKY

An empty sky of broken
dreams and shattered hope,
fills the world and all there
in.

The lightness of being, the
heaviness of lies. Crushed
existences, sin the victor,
evil it's tool.

Shared followers, wasted
grace, ignored redemption.
The blood of sacrifice washed
away by deluded thoughts.

THE MONSTER US

4 and 20 miles of earth this place called home.
Gold and silver everywhere. Food and drink
of every nation. This and more is offered to
those who will touch the heart of this monster.

It was a strange twist of fate that we arrived
here scared and alone. There is hatred in our
heart and tears in our soul.

There is one key to end this, if we are strong
enough. That key is love, but can we love this
hideous monster, when we can't even bear to
look upon its' face.

This monster is yourself, but it is no monster
at all. It is the truth about our self we can't face.
The truth that we are imperfect flawed creatures
who can and do extremely wonderful things and
also extremely horrendous things. God forgives
and loves us, so why can't we forgive and
love our self.

TONIGHT, TONIGHT

Where is your tomorrow?
Have you set it all out?
Could mistaken outcomes
be fate or chance?

Maybe if there was no
choice, but there is.

Tonight there's a party on
the roof, tonight there is
reason to celebrate, but will
tonight be a bonfire for you?
Hell that is.

Would tonight be better spent
preparing for Jesus' return?
That is unless your cold and
want a little heat.

TROUBLE

Trouble following too close. I
can't walk fast enough to get
away. Seems what's seen can
not be trusted to be sin free.

There's no confusion in Gods
world but I don't live there, yet.

Life can be a shell game, what
is thought to be an answer could
turn out to be wrong. Should we
give up, not play? Is that even a
possibility?

All I believe we can do is pray and
ask for Gods help because only he
knows the right answer.

UNSTOPPABLE

Put on earth with all its' beauty,
it should have been enough, but
we've filled it up with ugliness.
Now humans strive to live and
somewhere along the way some
of us began to care about each
other.

Oh I know there are some that
don't care for anyone but them
selves, but when shit hit's the fan,
the rest of us will be ready with
the toilet paper.

WILLFUL IS WRONG

Willful misdeeds, skillful but
false. Transfer excuses made
up in ways destined for
destruction. My way not yours.

Sent for the preacher called for
relief. Listened to the speech,
never let it in.

Said it best, when there was, a
reason to change. Now a
hardened heart refuses to
believe no other but selfish lies.

Wait before it ends, watchful
eyes can see mistaken ideologies.
Could it be as has been said, that
what was before deemed necessary
is still true.

WITHOUT YOU

I am lost, I am doomed, there's no way without you.
I am sure you're my hope, my salvation and my
shield rom the flames.

I am sure that you wait for me in your Heavenly home.
I will worship and I will praise your name in song.

On bended knees I will pray. With a humble heart I
will love.

In fear and doubt I will serve knowing you are the
only way.

All my now's, forever from this present now, I will
seek to make myself worthy of a room in your
home.

In death when I stand before your judgment throne,
I will wait, anxious for my eternal fate.

TO: CHRISTA RIMMER MY PRECIOUS GRANDCHILD

C---- CHERISHED
H----HEART
R----REVEALED
I----IN
S----SONG
T----TOLD
A----AND
R----REMEMBERED
I----IN
M----MAY
M----MY
E----EARTH
R----RULES

WRITTEN By Joy Olree

J----JUMP
O----ON
Y----YELLOW
O----OR
L----LET
R—Rotten
E----ESCAPE

JEALOUSY, HATE AND FEAR

As love lay sleeping hate crept in and stole the light,
while jealousy, and fear, shared things best meant
for others.

If ever there was a way to keep love safe, to banish
jealousy hate and fear, would we do it?

we are but servants of a higher power destined to
do the will of God.

If God created everything, did he also create jealousy
hate and fear, or are these just the byproducts of sin?

I can't be sure but whatever we must deal with jealousy
hate and fear in a Christian way.

Do what you will but as for me I will do the will of God
after I figure out what it is.

KEYS TO THE KINGDOM

Thank God it's Friday. Here's to the freaking weekend. 2 days until Sunday, 2 days until worship, singing and partaking of the Lords supper. Come to church one and all, see what God has in store for you. The Holy Ghost is waiting to fill you up and make it right. Raise the bar of religion, there's no need to be miserable, there's always hope

No matter what you do people are going to talk, God is going to watch, and life is too short.

I am going to church, hope to see you there. Got a smile on my face, love in my heart and a song on my lips. Going to get me some instruction, fellowship and encouragement. Got my mind on redemption and my hands on a Bible. Going to share by example put it all on my soul.

Everybody put your sin away, show the world your Jesus. He died for you won't you listen to what he has to say? Let life lead you to Heaven Not Hell.
The keys to the kingdom are within reach, will opportunity pass you by? He gave you a choice but he never said there would not be consequences for making the wrong choice. Hope to see you in church that is, but if I don't I'll wave at you from Heaven.

WHO DONE IT REALLY

Simple as it seems, complexities abound. That peanut butter on the fridge, the blood on the wall, French fries in the hair dryer, Crisco everywhere. Where's the beef you ask? Hamburger that is. Lemonade is so sticky covering the kitchen floor. Seems there used to be a cat in the house, now all I see are hairballs.

Mary, Mary quite contrary, what happened here? Okay screamed Mary, the alarm went off, I jumped up and stepped on a hairball and there was that cat sitting on the floor grinning like a Cheshire cat, so I went to swat it but hit a pitcher of lemonade instead. Then as lemonade splattered all over the floor, I backed into a knife covered with peanut butter sending it sailing into the air, landing on the fridge where it stuck.

To make a long story short, I was so frazzled, I decided to heat up some left over French fries in the microwave along with a veggie burger, but the ketchup would not come out of the bottle, so I hit it with my hand and ketchup went all over the wall.

I reached to grab a paper towel to wipe the wall but my feet got stuck k on the sticky lemonade covered floor and when I tried to pull myself free my hand hit a pot of Crisco on the stove and grease went grease went everywhere. How did the French fries get in the hair dryer, ask the cat and if you find him tell him there never was any beef, it was a vegie burger and I hope he choked on it.

CHANGE

Seems things have changed, been rearranged, added to and taken from. I wonder what God will say on judgment day when we try to explain what happened to his Bible. Does it not seem strange that humans think they know more than God when with one snap of his fingers all this could be destroyed. I bet won't nothing matter in the end because once we feel the fire of Hell it will be crystal clear we were wrong.

That old time religion done got replaced by something they call contemporary. Now I'm not sure exactly what that means except now they got a full band to go along with the piano. Funny how singing making melody in your heart got interpreted to drums, pianos and guitars. Last person I asked said, "well they had musical instruments in the old testament." They also sacrificed animals for sins. When was the last time a Baptist did that? And what about Pat Robinson, he says that marriage until death don't apply if your spouse has Alzheimer's because they are same as dead anyway..

Gee what's next sex in the pews, a little adultery and fornication for fellowship. We're already eating in the church building, calling it fellowship. Well my dictionary has a different definition then what most churches call fellowship.

I AM NOT STEPHEN KING

Self-publishing is a lot like trying to kiss your own ass, and not fart in the process. Every year most folks do what is called spring cleaning. It took me 50 years and 420 poems to get mine done, and I've already started filling the closet/computer back up.

I was born with clean hands but when I grew up I got caught with my hands in the cookie jar, sin that is, so I said, "God ain't going to want nobody in Heaven with cookie crumbs on their hands." Well 18 years later an aunt said, "of course God ain't going to want no one in Heaven with cookie crumbs on their hands, you better wash those hands." Well I got clean hands now but there are lots of cookie jars in the world and I love cookies, but if it be Gods will and with lots of hard work there it no Nabisco or Keebler going to keep me out of Heaven.

Enter John Barge and Brandon Drake. With their help and patience, now a book of my poetry has been published. Where I go from here is anybody's guess, but I truly believe if I had the money they could get me a night's stay in Oprahs' house. Self-publishing to date, about 5,000, holding a book containing 420 of my poems priceless.

I don't know who takes care of Mr. Kings business, and there ain't no dog foaming at the mouth, or no woman chained to a bed in some sex game, none of this is in my poems but I don't need any of that when I got me and someone like John Barge and Brandon Drake on my team.

POLITICS AND PIG STIES

Clean it up make it shine, rules and laws everywhere.
Speed up, speed over, slow down, cameras don't lie.

Safety in question, lives in the balance. Sure it's your
life, but you can't die until we say, and what if you kill
someone else? No that won't do.

106 can't be wrong, money, money, more, more. 8 days,
9 tickets, life is so unfair, and I'm a college graduate.
You say Ford I say Dodge, doctor, doctor, I have no
insurance. 88, 92, paid the ticket, not the meds, we
can't have it all.

Mistakes happen, laws exist can't pick and choose,
obey or pay. Still not happy? Curse the sky,
scream unfair, 50 dollars please.

A HIDDEN FAITH

Out of sight out of mind
important things are not
hidden.

Seems values have been
misplaced putting money
before faith.

What is the cost of an
invisible faith?

AN ETERNITY IN HELL.

A PASSING ANGEL

Oh death thou come so unexpected,
one hardly has time to prepare, but
even though I never knew you, I
know you were a passing angel, for
are we not all angels trapped in a
human shell waiting for death to
unwrap our wings.

A VALENTINE THOUGHT

A day of hearts as
designated by man.
Love grows, but it
is said to grow more
with a dozen roses
and a box of candy.

Who knew all it took
to seal the deal was
some chocolate and
flowers on February
fourteenth.

Makes me wonder if
Jesus would have fared
better if there had been
a Valentine's day back
then.

ALL I CAN BE

I am yet to be all I can be.
Opportunities avail with
choices to make, but my
finest hour is yet to be.

Lost but found, saved by
blood, tempted and tried.
Unworthy though I am,
victorious I will be, if
only I become all I can
be.

ARE WE F----- UP OR WHAT?

Colors swirl, light emits its glistening glow. Flawless caverns endless bottom existing in time, the seamless line of histories mistake. Fruitless bounties of famine and death, eaten bread of a baker's dozen. A penny for your thoughts, a dollar for a 4 o'clock scholar. Wish upon a fallen star, cast what's left of all processed on whatever is selling on HSN.

Simple though it may seem, nothing is ever as it looks. Pictures can confuse, reward or accuse. Hiding is a game where no place is secure and the terrorist knows the password before it's created. Election years are no different from any other year except more shit hit's the fan and there's less of us to clean it up.

How long will it be before we become another 3rd world country? Seems we're pretty close now. Pat Robinson says God has picked our next president, so maybe there's a chance we won't destroy ourselves before God does.

Babies, babies, everywhere is no one going to stop multiplying? The Duggers have 19 would have been 20 but fate stepped in. But don't go to sleep yet, they might still make 20, or would that be 21? Depends on whether you count a miscarriage as a child. But you'd better not go there unless you want the abortionist coming after you. I mean if miscarried babies are called people then what about aborted babies? Could be there's a lot of people getting killed in the USA., legally of course, but you know apples and oranges.

BITS AND PIECES

Bits and pieces, this and that. Sang for
your supper killed a bird.

Stepped on toes washed some clothes
Exercise, exercise, sure is tiring.
Do I eat to live or live to eat? Hungers
a bitch.

Sleep is good unless you're not sleepy.
Then it's a bitch too.
Visions of future dreams, what? Makes
no sense. Does anything make sense
or is life just a bitch?

Well I don't know, but I seem to
remember bits and pieces thrown
in the trash carried to the dump.
Hey that makes no sense either.
I'm going to bed I'm feeling
sleepy.

BLIND EYES THE EGOS TRICK

The boss thinks:
Better than others, smarter too.
Did you touch that? Help I pay
to abuse you. Created equal in
what reality? Did you really
think life would be fair?

The conscience says to the boss:
Ego addict keep your eyes opened.
oh yea I forgot you are blinded by
your self-righteous bullshit.

Listen up a trick has been played
and the jokes on you. The ego got
you thinking some soul destroying
stuff. You are no better or smarter
then anyone. Your shit stinks and
your and your soul are going straight
to Hell if you don't listen to God.

Then the boss thinks:
Maybe it's time for a change, and
he gets dressed and goes to church.
The end????????????????????? Not.

CARE DEFERRED

Hunger and poverty
seems the norm. Is
it possible to care
with all the wrong
in our lives?

A dollar here, is worth
more there, then it will
ever mean to us.

I guess if we can deny
our creator it is easy to
deny the hungry in places
we may never see except
in ad on TV.

CHRISTMAS IN THE WORLD

Last night as you put your turkey in the oven to cook
several thousand children died from starvation.
This morning as you open your presents
someone's child is sleeping in a cardboard box.
I say all this not to depress anyone but to make you
aware of how blessed you are.

If I could have one wish granted this Christmas season
it would be for each and of us to take a close look at
our lives and to see how blessed we are and ask
ourselves is there something I could do for the less
fortunate.
God had one son that he loved, but because he also loved
us his creation, he sent his son to die for our sins. This
Christmas please thank him and if you have anything you
don't need please give it to someone who can use it.

There is a Heaven waiting for all who want it but do we
want it as bad as we want the latest video game? Is
there anything on earth more important than a home with
God? Would you risk an eternity in Hell for anything?

COLD LOVE

Beneath Heaven
in the dessert of
fallen souls,
there lived a child
of fire. Her heart a
stone spring from
which flowed no
love.

Was in an eternal
night that she woke
to see a wooden man.
Unwritten, implied
emotions filled her
soul.

It could have been a
beautiful friendship
but tears of the sun
fell until nothing
was left but the
shadow of cold love.

CREATIVE MUSINGS

Sound evades a noiseless scheme. Flow of energy an inner child its woven pattern complex but sure.
Follies compete through endless eons and eras of pointless stuff. An actor's school, creative fantasy
for sheltered idiots of humankind.

Creatures beware gold and silver allure but with time, It seems there ought to be some gain In truth, but floods of persuasive lies drown what hope that should insure a peaceful existence. Systems endowed to protect life are cluttered with viruses and spam. Crowded landfills, cities and towns share tragedies destined to destroy a future generations right to live.

If there were means to solve life's drama, reality TV would give it a spot on Saturday Night Live
and a lifetime of reruns destined to pacify all concerns, making no difference but allowing us to die with a smile on our poverty ridden faces.

Presidential candidates sling mud faster than Mr. Clean can unscrew his cap. Pancakes anyone?
Filibusters and lobbyist want our support but with most of the voting age folks either not registered or else can't read, does it matter what anyone wants? Picture please. Who are you? It don't matter if you are a hundred, photo id required to vote.

Once upon a time, happy ever after and all that b--s we had a chance, but technology got invented an Steve Jobs created the I-pad and everybody went crazy trying to be the next You Tube sensation and what's better today will be obsolete tomorrow. But hey God has not changed ever. Makes you wonder if maybe we are barking up the wrong tree.

CRUSHED

Had a sister, wanted a brother, and got one for 7 days. Crushed.
Had a mother, and a father, grandparents too. Mom died at 37,
I was 16. All the rest followed, dad died at 79, I was 55. Crushed.

I had a son married soon after, had a daughter, got abused,
got a divorce. Crushed. Along came husband number 2, a
father figure. I got tired of being the daughter so I divorced
him too, but not before having daughter number 2 crushed.

Now I have husband number 3, my soul mate. He wants to run
but love has him chained just like me. Crushed.
1 child, 2 child, 3 child, 1 husband, 2 husband 3 husband, me,
my worst enemy. Crushed.

DEATH BY ASSOCIATION

It's true I knew, but chose
a blind eye. Could a
mistake have been made
a mistake unto death?

What can I say in the end,
when I stand in the presence
of God? Will I'm sorry keep
me from Hell?

Is a word fitly spoken really
like apples of gold in a silver
box? If so then depart I know
you not must be the cost of
spiritual blindness.

DEATH WILL NOT CLAIM ME

I can't stop this feeling.
Where ever I may be
I refuse destruction
over life. Death will
not claim me as long
as faith is inside my
HEART.

EMPATHY FOR THE SON

I hear feelings in my sleep,
feel the nails in my soul.
The courage it must have
taken, the love he must
have had for his father, to
die for me.

Can I ever be worthy of
such a sacrifice? Is it even
mine to hope?
Day in day out working on
my salvation. Every minute
knowing this could be my
last chance to please God.

One moment the son will
Will my service be deemed
acceptable? This I pray as
I cry with empathy for the
son. Gods son, my savior.

EMPTY ROOM

Empty rooms, fallen eves,
cracked paint like the bruised
lives of childless couples.

Empty realities threaten truth
and meaning. Shallow depths,
existence frail.

Translucent design hidden in a
dreamers dream turned to dust
with time and rust.

Present existences end with eternal
futures, a non-existent fact, based
on faith.

Unseen, reality may seem,
one thing is sure, today, tomorrow,
now, we will face it ready or not.

ELDER FOLKS

Elder folks, ask
for so little, yet
gave so much
in wisdom, time
and love.

Called over the
hill, but if not
for them, there
would be no us.

MY IT, MY GOD

You are the one God, my it, my
salvation. May I never feel your
wrath. May I worship with fear
and humility knowing your son
died for me and without him I
would have no hope.

FARAWAY

Faraway amongst
the stars angels sing.
Faraway a palace
waits its design divine.
Faraway where love
abounds and God is king,
and Jesus sits,
there waits a home
for all, who've chose
to give up sinful things.

FEAR-FAITH

How much faith removes fear?
Can it be known if decisions
are right when the judge does
not talk to you? What kind of
research will keep a soul from
trembling?

When the purpose is pleasing
God, but doubt makes it unclear
if God is pleased, where can
answers be found?

Faith with a little hope mixed
in, it seems is all we have, but
maybe it is all we need.

Fear is real and so is faith, maybe
with the two of them I will
get into Heaven.

FEAST OR FAMINE

Chicken and potatoes we have,
a cup of rice, a sip of water,
So little they ask for, another
day of life the hunger pains
to leave.

Soon a Heavenly home will
be theirs but woo to these
humans that feasted while
Gods little children died
from a famine they did not
create.

Could you not spare a dollar
to feed a starving child? I guess
we know the answer to that one
because Jesus ask for a sip of
water and got vinegar.

Wake up people see the horror
around you before Jesus comes
and personally opens your eyes.

FLY, FLY, FLY

To soar to unimaginable heights is my goal,
but it is often hard to see how a sinner like
me can hope to defeat someone like the Devil
but I try every day, because there is something
inside me that won't let me give up.

Now I won't know the outcome of this war
until I stand before the judgment seat of God,
but when the roll is called up yonder I'll be
there waiting to see if my name is in the book
of life.

And if life has not passed when Jesus comes
again, I hope will flyyyyyyyyy to my eternity.

FOREIGN AFFAIRS GET ME BY

Chosen rules thrown out fools,
careless shoes sing the blues.
Simple it comes, for men deny
anything there was to reply.

Were they ever going to make
it right. Their excuses are fake.
All efforts reduced to lame
attempts at the gratification of
life's stark realization that what's
believed might just as well be a
fairytale for all the good it does
them.

This tried and failed, hit or miss,
games we play would seem to be
a foreign affair to get us by until
with time the facts are faced that
God is true and we just might be
doomed.

GOD CAN YOU LEND US A HAND?

What can be believed in when it all seems hopeless? I thought I knew the truth, thought I had everything to gain and nothing to lose. First my brother, then my mother, now my father, what do you want God? Haven't I given enough? Does your son's blood require all that I have? I don't want to be angry, but I don't understand why you sit in Heaven and watch as we destroy ourselves and all you created. God will you please lend us a hand? We sure pray a lot, pay lots of dues, give up lots of stuff, all because of your promise of a better life in Heaven. All this is hard to believe when your belly is hungry and death is all around and your body hurts from sickness and old age.

Now don't get me wrong I love you and your son, I just don't understand why it seems you choose not to help us. I know we killed your son but our sons are killed every day. Mothers and fathers killing children, only we just have to take it because revenge is sin.

Then there's that Hell thing, yeah that place sounds real scary. one bundle of pain forever, now that's a long time with no Tylenol. The worse thing here on earth is nothing compared to Hell.

But why does it have to be that way? I read you got a temper. In the Old Testament not even Moses, as much as you liked him could not keep from messing up at least once. It seems once is all it takes when you get angry. As long as there is life in my body I will try to please you, but God could you please lend me a hand?

GUARANTEES

Can't deny the way it feels.
Can't say the truth is wrong.
Found there was more to
prospects of eternity then
was known.

Wish definitions came with
absolutes. Trust to reveal
fear and doubt. Came to
benefit from knowledge and
wisdom.

With endings come judgments
and beginnings, but to believe
in guarantees would seem to
put oneself in place of God.
Something which could not
be done

MY THANKSGIVING GIFT TO YOU

Oh turkey so golden brown, pumpkin pie sweet and orange. "I thirst," he said. Dressing and cranberry sauce, giblet gravy and sweet potato casserole. What a feast today. Why even the poorest among us could have a Big Mac at McDonalds "I thirst, he said."

As we get dressed for the holiday celebrations, do we ever think about the one who died for us? When you put earrings through the holes in your ears do you ever see the wooden nails being driven in his innocent hands? If you wear a hat do you ever see the thorny crown on his head?

I thirst, "he said." a little water was all he wanted but what he got was vinegar. Laughter and mocking, a heavy cross to bear, a death to endure his reward for healing the sick and raising the dead.

"Father if it be your will let this cup pass from me, but not my will yours," he cried.

Who among us would stand still, while beaten, nails driven in our body and not put up a fight? And who among us if given the chance would not seek revenge.

"I thirst, he said." but all he got was vinegar. As the sky darkened and his life neared its end he cried, "Father forgive them for they know not what they do."

Then did Jesus die and 3 days later was risen alive. So as you eat your holiday meal, even if only a Big Mac, remember the innocent man, Jesus who died for you

HEARTLESS WONDERS

Heartless wonders of creation, stiff--necked know-it-alls,
why could you not see. The miracles were there, he
stood right before you, gave all he had, but still you
would not believe.

A crown of thorns a cross to carry, ridiculed and
mocked vinegar to drink yet with his last breath he
loved us.

Father he cried, "Forgive them for they know not what
they do" A mother wept as friends deserted. Yet on
the third day he arose alive.

God how could you stand it, to watch your son sacrificed
for such as we. I wish there could have been another
way but when I turn on the television all I hear is hate
and death, making it clear, without your son's death we all
would be doomed.

HELP

My eyes see beauty, my soul longs to sin.
Strength can't be found in a bottle or court
of law. Temptation moves like fine wine,
a soft melody, a pleasant taste, sweet to
the tongue, bitter to the soul.

Evil arises clothed in desire. Waiting, seeming
harmless, but interest in forbidden things
threatens the eternal damnation of our soul.

To worship earthly creations while ignoring
the beauty of God and his promise of Heaven
could be deadly on judgment day.

Help exists, in the Bible. Help can free a soul,
but help is not forever, it dies when we do, as
does the opportunity we had to please God.

Get it right while there is life in your physical
body and you won't be wrong in Gods' eyes.

HOPE WITH LIFE

To rise above limits set by man.
To refuse to see benefits of sin.
To worship even in the face of
death and destruction.

To know and believe in hope
as long as there is life. To
follow with faith in the mist
of doubts.

Oh Lord hear my prayer, for
I am a sinner in need of hope
with life.

HERO FOR ALL

When a hero comes along,
do we not stand and worship?
Yet Gods son Jesus, the greatest
hero to ever come, we crucified
on a cross between two thieves.

HOPE

I live to ascend
Fear to conquer.
Hell to avoid,
Heaven to win.

Hope is all I have
but it may be all I
need.

HOPELESS PLACE

Sin surrounds, hate threatens.
Where is faith in a hopeless
place? How can it be said
love died for me when I am
so full of rage?

HOPELESS

Hopeless I am not, useless never, because God don't make no junk. Helpless I was until God sent his son to die for me. Where there was dark there is now light.

When I am scared I pray. When I need friends I visit the folks at the nursing home.

They don't get around so good, and their eyes and ears may be weak, but their love is strong.

Never much cared for folks, seemed they never much cared for me, but with the ladies and gentlemen at the nursing home I feel right at home.

Death will come for us all, when and where can't be known but I know one thing, I am not hopeless and boy do I have friends.

HUMILITY IS MINE

Take what's left
of all I have, for
all I need is God.

Use my service lord
if it be your will, for
I am yours.

I HAD LOVE, NOW I GIVE LOVE

Born in love cherished and loved. Cared for physically and spiritually.
Given knowledge of a fathers love, a love so strong that he gave his only
son to die for me.

Now I grieve my own mother gone too soon. My father followed
40 year later, but I had love. Maybe not the same kind of love that
God had for his son Jesus but close I'm sure.

Now I care for the mother that married a man with 3 kids and
little money, but I have love. Fate does indeed have a strange
twist sometimes but I had love and now I give love.

I can't say I'm perfect because we know that's not possible,
but I can say that I had love and now I give love. One day I shall
stand before God and hopefully he will say I've done to please
him, but whatever I had love and now I give love.

I KNOW IT ALL

The philosophy of know it all, a breeding ground for disaster.
Simple and complete, my way or the highway.

Feel confusion feel despair feel the pointlessness of debating
the truth with hard headed, your mistaken, kind of fellows.
Could it not be argued the Jews were of this mind set? Did
they not feel Jesus and even Paul was wrong.
When will and what will it take for humans to realize, they
are not in charge and it does not matter one bit what they
think about anything pertaining to God.

We have been given a Bible, stating exactly what God
expects of us and the only thing we can do it read it
and try to do what God wants and hope he is pleased
with what we do.

I THINK THEREFORE

Bullshit, what does it matter what I think?
I could be wrong and probably are. Now
where do I go from here?

Once upon a time I was born and now I
wait for death and judgment. Seems well,
I'd better get to reading and praying and
hoping because Heaven is where my father
lives and Hell is where no one wants to live,
but lots of folks are going to live if they don't
do what God wants them to.

And then she died and went to Heaven and
lived happily ever after, the end.

IF ONLY

Fastened strategies
unsung heroes, a
mile a minute the
broken rule. Former
things are passed
away.

Creations change
would be, a blessed
response to sin and
strife, if only humans
were willing to give
up their desire for sin

INNOCENCE

I came an innocent child to live a life until death, to fight
to conquer to thrive to fly to rise to flyyy Give the Devil
his due I came to win to flyy. No moment of time can
erase a sinner's folly but heavenly blood is stronger
than the finest soap. Man can do so much but not
enough to change his fate without God on his side.

Countries struggle and fall, sin flourishes and kills,
people scream and fear worship idols and false
prophets, but God watches and waits hoping his
creation will obey his commands.

what parent would not want the best for their
child? And what parent would not punish
a child that disobeyed them. And what parent
would not forgive a child that sincerely ask
for forgiveness. How much more is the same,
not true for our Heavenly father.

Oh sinners hearken to the call of salvation for
without it there is no hope for anything but
a pit of fire.

INSTRUCTIONS IN HOPE

Give me all I need, leave fate to your discretion.
Send clear instructions for to follow.

My rest assured in hope of eternal promise

Once saved, fell back now I'm on the right track
hoping to get kind words from you God.

Some would say once saved always, but you
and I know the sinner inside.

Probabilities are sure to lead astray if for
one minute I think I know more than you.

Judgments are yours, fulfillments mine
but hope guarantees that I will keep
trying to gain a home in Heaven.

INTERNATIONAL LOVE

Sent from our father. Our last hope, and
we crucified him on a cross.

Is there any reason to deserve Heaven?
Yes there is because Jesus had international,
universal love for us.

A Grammy he never won, a Pulitzer neither
but then he never hit a woman. He never
hit anyone. His only crime, if that's what the
Jews chose to call it, was being perfect.

I am not perfect and I sin every day, but if
Whitney is in Heaven, here I come MS and all.

IS ANYBODY AFRAID OF THE DEVIL ANYMORE

I remember a time when folks feared the Devil, they weren't out here
killing, stealing, fornicating and other sinning.
You know sin don't look like it did Las Vegas sure looks inviting,
Britney Spears is just a young girl. A sexy dressing drinking
young girl, but a mother of 2 little boys. It seems with birth
control readily available, even fornication is no big deal.

I know a man says he has always felt bad because he is not gay,
he said, "in Hollywood, gay people get all the perks."

They use to say crime don't pay, but let them convict the wrong fellow
and after he sues and wins millions, you won't say crime don't pay. With a
good lawyer and enough money you can get away with murder. The only
ones getting punished these days are the poor and powerless.

I don't believe the actual Devil is running around causing folks to sin but
he sure has a lot of people doing his dirty work for him.
Here is the truth, if you don't fear the Devil, then you better get ready
to spend an eternity in Hell., because that's just were you might end up.
The Devil, or rather his influence, whatever you want to call it, is bad and
be afraid or one day he just might become your friend.

JOY OLREE

J---Just
O---Only
Y---Your
O---One
L---Life
R---Role
E---Enter
E---End

JUDGMENTS ARE WRONG

They call you fat, they call you thin,
confidence will cease to begin, for
all they see is the first layer of skin,
instigating your future decent.

Enjoy your wealth, enjoy your dimes.
Destroy everything beautiful you find.
No one ever gets rich by being kind,
and there are two sides to every glory.

I'll call your bluff every time and I
hope to God you call mine, for there's
no way we're all blind, and I resent
every judgment.

Don't forget your killers mind. Don't
ignore to help ignite, for its only
separated by a remorseless grind, and
there are two sides to every story.

VIRGINIA LAK

V----Various
I----Innocent
R---Rug rats
G----Get
I---Inside
N----Now
I----I'm
A----A
L----Little
A----Angry
K----Kid

LIBERAL LIBERTARIANS

One word, one book, ten thousand or more
              interpretations.

God says" jump." we say, "with or
without shoes?" God says, "fellowship,"
we say," ok but it's better with food,"

God says, "you can't enter Heaven except
you be as a little child." We say," so let
us build a playground for the children."

Revelations says, "To not take or add
anything." We say," The Bible doesn't say
the church can't do this, so it must be ok."

Liberal thinking seems to be the way of
Christianity today, but could libertarian
ways keep us out of Heaven?

God judges but remember he punished
the angels that sinned.

LOVE BLOOMS

Loves blooms its fragile state.
Hate descends destruction to
vanquish all traces of care and
compassion.

When saints and sinners fight
to live it must be time to let
God in.

Can't deny life will be forever,
can't forget it will not be in
this present form.

Without the love of God for his
creation future eternity would
be a living Hell.

Keep the faith, there is hope,
for God our father has a home
prepared for all who let love bloom
for him and his son who died for us.

LOVE BY BIRTH

Born of love,
lived in love,
died in love.

Resurrected
in love to
return in
love.

MEANINGS

Dead means dead.
Hate means hate.
Love means love.
All words mean
something.

Face value always
the best way to
look at any word.

Putting our own
meanings to words
tends to confuse,
the listener, because
they can't tell if we
are lying or telling
the truth.

MINE

Mine is not yours.
Taken in due time.
Future requests
deemed necessary
to ensure profitable
outcomes.

Tick tock the clock
ticks, seconds to
minutes, minutes to
hours. A life of time
spent in this or that.

Time would seem
endless at best, yet
one day it will stop.
Then mine will be
Gods' as it always
was.

Enough of selfishness,
share as time allows,
before selfish ways
become a sin.

MS_ NORM

What's always been
seems the norm, till
what's always been
decides to change,
and not for good.

Then comes a doctor
who changes what's
always been, so what
once was thought the
norm becomes a lie.

NO MEANING

Walking desert plains,
wondering the meaning
of it all, there arises a
thought that maybe there
is no meaning just a reality
I won't accept.

The reality that maybe things
are as they are because we
have rejected God.

OCCUPY, OCCUPY

Take my hand help me stand, follow nothing lead nowhere.
Occupy, occupy, where's the problem now? Wall Street
New York, LA., the world, is anyone happy?

Seems there has to be some drama, or else we'd have
to go to church. I mean how can we worship God when
the big boy are getting rich and the rest of us can't
afford to eat Chinese.

Grow your own food, seriously, with McDonalds on
every street corner. Hey Cher has a different outfit
for every day, I just want some clothes to cover my
body every day. Thousands of dollars she spends for
clothes that barely covers her body but don't dare
try to touch her.

Scream if it works, but it probably won't. Wal-Mart is
king and it's foolish to shop there. We save money
and Wal-Mart gets rich. Why no occupy there? Well
then we'd have to shop at Dollar General. Wouldn't
that be awful saving money on stuff we really needed.
Maybe we'd better occupy the Bible so we won't need
to occupy anything else.

PEACE FOR A SOUL

Forever there is doubt.
Forever there is love.
Endings guaranteed
judgment assured.
Fallacies my demise
temptation the thorn
in my side.

Thin lines separate sin
from Godliness, but 'tis
a vast divide between
Heaven and Hell.

Task at hand to be done.
Rest at the close of
finished goals. Safety
accomplished with doubt,
and hope.

Wish there was peace for
a soul, but until I hear God
say enter in my good and
faithful servant, there will
be none

SIMPLE IS BEST

Simple is always best,
but complicated is the
norm by which many
are deceived.

Bright lights and fancy
words can blind us into
thinking that whatever
we want is ok with God.

Gut wrenching emotional
drama seems to quell the
need to be anything but a
nameless number in a sea
of misguided individuals
bent on saving themselves
from whatever they don't
feel is important.
Sure it might be great if that
was the answer but first we'd
have to conquer God, and if
you've read the Bible you'll
see it's was tried and God
won.

RISE

Stand to rise
above the drama.
Pray for help to
understand Holy
words.

Keep sleep away
to be ready when
the bridegroom
comes.

Fear the sinner
inside. Keep
watchful eyes on
it before it acts
out foolish desires.

SIN AND ME

Angels and conflict, devils and sin.
why is there not an easier way to
serve God?
Human we are, and sinful our cross to
carry. Could desire not look so harmless?
Would it not be better to be a monk in a
cave?
Go into all the world was the command.
Teach my doctrine, give hope to the lost.
Guess that means the monk cave thing is out.
Oh well there would have been spiders in
the cave anyway and I'm scared of spiders.

Ok sin do your worse, I got God on my side,
maybe I can keep me out of trouble without
having to cut off a hand or pluck out an eye.
Gosh why does sin look so good sometimes?

SIN IS NO FRIEND

Sin is not my friend,
death is not the end.
Eternity is a long time.
Hell is a fiery nightmare
where no one wakes up.

Heaven is a paradise
created for Christians.
A reality so wonderful
it might seem a dream
but no one wants to wake
up.

Heaven-Hell your choice.
Friend-foe, sin is no
friend.

SOMEONE LIKE ME

Sinner I am, sinner I'd stay,
sinner I'd die, and to Hell
I'd go, except for the blood
of an innocent man, for
someone like me.

STOP THIS MADNESS

Insanity rules, it's
master the Devil.
Did we not once
have a savior? Oh
yea we did but we
crucified him on a
cross.

But he loved us so
much with his last
words he ask his
father to forgive us.

Maybe we should
stop and think,
before someone
hangs us on a
cross.

THE DEVILS BEST FRIEND

You ever see bad luck that wanted good?
Seems misery really does love company.
Enter the Devil. Now he has friends, but
they are in Hell just like him. So in order
to prove a point, at least to God, he has
decided to bring as many people as he can
down to Hell with him.

The Bible says you will know a tree by the
fruit it bears, but put on your glasses to see
what kind of fruit you are looking at.

The blind lead the blind unless you first
put on shades to keep out the light from
the flames of Hell.

Remember this, a fallen man will not fall
because he is already down, but humans
high on themselves will fall every time.

THE DRAGON OF RAINBOW COLORS

In a faraway land lived a dragon of rainbow colors.
He could not fly or breathe fire so all he did was sing.
This would have been an excellent thing but his
voice was gruff, and the children ran away when they
heard him sing. This of course made him cry. There
seemed no way to resolve this problem when from the
East there came a little girl grown of midnight longings
and desperate wishes.

Fearless she was having long ago lost everything there
was to want. To this dragon she came with a flute
plucked from the vine of hope. She played a tune and
bade the dragon to sing. With reluctance he complied
and to his amazement his voice which had once been
gruff was now soft and sweet.

This song filled the air and soon the land was filled
with children and their families who clapped and
danced until the wee morning hours. Was at the break
of dawn, that tired and happy everyone went home to
bed and sleep dreaming of a dragon of rainbow colors
with the voice of an angel.
The lesson if there is one, is with hope all things are possible.

TONIGHT IS THE BEGGING

Up front best seats, house seats, money gives increase. Car in the parking lot, tuxedo rented. All for the good of one thing or another. Charity it's called, begging more true. Money to ease your conscience. Send in the accountants, to seal the deal tax free.

Tonight is music, stars and ass kissing. We should know by now the truth can't be bought. Is there ever going to be love of one another just because it's right

One day we may beg for our soul but it will be too late. Tonight, now, beg for help in understanding what is needed so there will be no begging at the feet of God.

UH OH

Colossal mistakes, can be unto
death, unless forgiven
by asking through Jesus, Gods
son.

Sin, unavoidable, is not deadly
unless viewed as harmless.

With life there is hope, but in
death all hope dies with us.

A TRAPPED SOUL

Trapped in my demise sheltered from all hope.
Cared not for promises of faith.

Comfort and desire seems to sooth the body
but does little for the soul.

God in all his glory sent his only son, destined
to die at the hands of his own creation.

Sinner that I am, I turned my back on Jesus
and his father.
Years went by finding no rest in me. Scared
and crying I came before your church begging
for forgiveness.

My Bible says God can't lie and it says God
hears the sincere prayer of a righteous soul
and her I am.

UNCOMMON KNOWLEDGE

Sinners beware your knowledge is faulty.
Users abuse issues of faith. Taken apart
added to, and confused made to suit
personal desires. Failures of understanding
destines to destroy.

Uncommon it may seem, this Heavenly
knowledge but in truth it has been before
the beginnings of time. Yet did man refute
it as though it were a lie, preferring instead
to create his own version of the truth.

Sinners make sure, for your sins will find you,
when standing before the throne of God. Then
will uncommon knowledge be the key to your
destruction.

UNDERSTANDING EXISTENCE

Deep within human existence lies
the seed of purposefulness.

Aspirations of potential life beyond
physical confines.

Standing above defeat, hands raised
in surrender to Heavenly power.

Day one-day end, the in-between,
preparing for future eternities.

WE NEED A HERO

We needed a hero.
We had a hero but
we refused him.
Ooooooooooooooh.

We still need a hero.
We still have a hero,
and Jesus is his name.
Ooooooooooooooh.

Cleansing blood,
blood of innocence,
shed for an unworthy,
selfish, chosen people.
Ooooooooooooooooh.

When will we learn
that what's best for us
is not always what we
want.
Ooooooooooooooooh.

WITHOUT YOU

Fire and pain, gnashing of teeth
without you.

Never again to see my mother
or my father, without you.

Grandparents, aunts and uncles,
a 7 day old brother, all gone
forever without you.

What can this world ever offer
that compares with what I have
already lost?

Say whatever, it's freewill, but I
know what God wants and I know
what I want, and I can't have it
without you.

Innocent, Jesus came innocent, he
died, but to the last breath he loved
us and to my last breath I will love
him and be thankful for without him
I would have no hope.

A DRINKERS LAMENT

How much liquor does it take to put out the fires of Hell?
In a drunken stupor I woke up in Hell, burning beyond
description. How I got here I don't know. I don't recall
dying, but I do remember taking another drink.

Frantically, in pain, I search for a way out of here. I beg
for help, but there is none. Resigned to an eternity in
Hell, I scream as fire burns a body unable to burn.

How much is your soul worth? Well, Jesus, the son
of God, died for your soul.

Maybe a bottle of whiskey will boost the economy,
maybe a bottle of whiskey will ease your human pain,
but a bottle might also send you to Hell.

Is it worth it? Let your soul decide then vote no.

A FALLEN ANGEL

A fallen Angel waits in Hell as
a risen Savior waits in Heaven.
A fallen Angel gathers troops,
his home prepared, a risen
Savior gathers souls, his home
prepared.

A fallen Angel nor his troops
offer hope, but a risen Savior
is the hope of righteous souls.

A MINDS MUSINGS

Through to leanings,
thought before,
now is gone.

The seen beginnings,
new and strange,
but true.

Its' pure rewards for
living life Gods' way.

A MINUTES LAST PLEA

Colors swirl,
fall and die,
'tis a minutes
last request
for summer
to stay.

AND THE WORLD WILL KNOW YOUR NAME

Nameless child son of a carpenter, son of God, born of a virgin,
innocent of sin, yet hung on a cross to die for MY sins.
Unselfishly he taught his father's commands knowing it would
mean his death. A death he was born for. With the faith of a
son for his Heavenly father, he gave his life for God's creation,
humanity.

No Pulitzer, Grammy, no Nobel Peace Prize, though he deserved
them all. Never inducted into the Hall Of Fame, but his name
shall be known by every human that ever lived.

Called a liar, and a blasphemer all lies. Called king of the Jews
and a Heavenly king he was. He could have called 10,000 angels,
to end his suffering but instead he died for ME.

A mother wept, a father watched, as humanity hardened their
hearts and the son of God was crucified..

One day, the world will know his name and every knee will bow,
but not all will rejoice most will beg for mercy, and there will be
none.

AS LONG AS GOD LOVES ME

Taking chances, seen the
limits. Foolish beginnings,
failed mistakes, destined
for greatness.

Going nowhere, came a
slave. Sin the lock, God
the key.

Trials and tragedy cover
the soul. No way out it
would seem, but victory
is mine, as long as God
loves me.

AS LONG AS YOU LOVE ME

Let them come, send
their worst, what can
they do to me as long
as you love me?

Death the reality of
human realms, but
matters not in Gods'
Heaven where is no
death.

Life is hard, suffering
severe, but endurance
the key to here ever
after.

Let it descend until
only the soul remains.
Let Hell scream for me
as loud as it can, but I
will not go as long as
you love me.

BEEN AND DONE

Can't worry about what's been and done.
Futures are the now and do. What is the
answer to the dilemma? The religious
quandary of right and wrong.

God created, sent his son to teach us, we
hardened our hearts, me, me, me. My will
not his, the norm by which it seems we live.

Mega million is our God, deceit and vanity,
the egos instruments of control. In a another
reality there might be hope, but in this
Godless world we have destroyed the Devil
and he has become a harmless fairy tale.

But there is still a remnant of God fearing
Christians who love God and his son Jesus,
and who spend their lives doing the will of
God. It is these humans, when all has been
and done, will receive their just reward, a
home in Heaven.

DARKNESS AND LIGHT

On a hill of death at Satan's behest,
was prophecy fulfilled, and darkness
seemed to win.

But on the 3ʳᵈ day light fulfilled its'
prophecy and mans' salvation was
assured.

DEATH

Death is for the living, grief their bitter pill.

Swallowed down with tears longing for
relief.

Money for the profit destined to ensure.

Life a bitter struggle preparing for its end.

Together is the hope God and all his glory.

Satan's ever lurking, luring with his tricks.
Resistance is the key, death the beginning.

Promises made, given to the faithful.
All is as it should be, life, death, eternity

DIAMONDS

Is there anything more beautiful than Gods love for
me? A love so great he sent his son to die for me.

Cherished diamonds, one we call Hope. It is said
the diamond has the sharpest cutting edge.

If Heaven used these words, then Jesus is the
Hope diamond, the sharpest cutting edge sin
has ever seen.

God loves the world more than any human
could love a diamond. His love eternal and
guaranteed, if only we put him first.

Jesus, Gods' son loved us so much, he willingly
died for our sins.

I am but a beggar in a rich man's world of
sin, but there is a home waiting for me in
Heaven.

DON'T GIVE UP ON ME

Lord knows I've been a mess.
Lord knows I've done my sin.
Lord knows I'm human to the
core.

Lord knows my weakness and
my strength, but for all my
faults the lord knows my heart.
So this I say, "please don't
give up on me for I won't give
up on you."

DON'T WAKE ME UP

If this love is not real, if my struggles are
pointless, don't wake me up. If Gods son
did not die for me, if Heaven is a Disney
movie, don't wake me up. If my prayers
are just words, if my Bible just a book,
don't wake me up.

Life is real and my faith is real, and I am
awake, because Gods love is real. All my
struggles have a point. God's son did die
for me. The Bible is non-fiction, and God
does hear my prayers.

One day, I hope to enter a real Heaven that
even Disney could not imagine.

FIGHTING FOR HEAVEN

Give me poverty, give me pain,
trials and tribulations. Give me
all earth's got, but at Heavens
gate the angels will be singing
here comes a fighter, welcome.

HUMANITY

Discarded humanity, its'
unremembered human
kind.

Swallowed up in darkness
switched, torn, trashed.
Journalist verify the known
but forgotten.

Ignorance runs rampant while
truth and justice die a slow
death, trampled under false
prophets.

Ends come, but rewards few as
humanity realizes mistakes
too late.

I CAN ONLY IMAGINE

Earths treasures give much pleasures, joy beyond measure,
but I have read of a place, beauty as has never been seen.

Wonder amazes this human. What could something
like this look like? My mind fills with images, pictures,
creations based on my known.

Then I pause for life calls and in truth I can only
imagine what Heaven would be like.

Today, tomorrow, forever, I hope to one day
see this beautiful place in person, then it will
not only be my imagination, it will be my home.

Surrounded by my mothers and father,
grandparents and friends it will be the fulfillment
of a life's work.

But for now I can only imagine and pray.

PRAY

Thankful for all tears
grateful for all feelings.
Time was, I did not feel,
a time when emotions
never came.

Now I cry like a baby
at ever little tragedy.

Seems everything was
thoughts in poetic form,
but life's no poem and
tragedy real.

People hurt, hearts break,
now I feel it. What once
was stone is sponge soft.

f God in his glory could
get his people to feel as I
do now, maybe things
would be better.

IDLENESS

Idleness concludes,
meaning to do,
wasted on time,
fretted away in
periods of quiet.

I'M SO GLAD

I'm so glad you came,
created me in your
image, gave me hope
of eternity in your
Heaven.

I'm so sorry we didn't
give your son more
respect. It was so
selfless for him to
die for us sinners.

I'm not sure we will
ever be worthy of
your love but I'm
sure this one, me
will go to her grave
trying to prove her
love for you.

IMAGINE

Think about fairies, think about rainbows
everything Disney imagined, all rolled up
in one day of fun.

Think of where you'd be if only there was
a way to get there. Think of world peace,
no homelessness or hunger.

Think of love, then think of God. Think of
a newborn baby wrapped up in pink, think
of boys and girls dressed in their Sunday
best.

Think of all you'd lose if you let sin win,
think of an eternity without the only one
who truly loves you.

Think on all these things, then imagine
YOU, standing tall, looking sin in the eye
and saying to Hell with you, I'm going to
Heaven.

JESUS CHRIST IS NOT RUNNING FOR PRESIDENT

It is a presidential election year,
and the fight is on.

Let me state the truth, Jesus
Christ is not running, and He
is the only perfect person that
has ever lived, so there will be
no perfect person running for
president.

We can vote for the person we
feel will do the least damage to
our country, and we can pray.

LIGHTS OF LOVE

Show me lights, send invites,
chase away dreams. Liquid
enhanced lies, smoke filled
drama, equate to the max.

Illusions of false promise.
Chance encounters of win.
A sinners delusion. Forbidden
sin washed in cloned blood.
Lighten speeds of demise, a
soul killer.

Without love there is death. To
love others as self, the greatest
command, second only to love
for God and Jesus Christ.

LOVES TIMES TWO

1 plus 1 is 2, love times 2 is God's blessing on a mothers' heart.
Uncertainty rules this human existence, but the certainty of
God's love quells the bitterest of trying times.

In the heart of unrest and trouble, a miracle reveals itself,
the birth of a soul. God creates man enjoys.

Can I find joy in this life, so new and innocent as I struggle
to understand why Gods son had to die for me?

It seems not meant for understanding, but one fact has
revealed itself, because this man died for me, I have
hope and on this day, April 1, 2013 there is a soul
destined for birth and a grandmother dedicated to one
say Thank you Jesus.

This Poem was written while watching a video
of my unborn grandchild, sent to me from Georgia,
by the mother, my daughter, Virginia Lak.

MADNESS

Death is for the living, grief their bitter pill. Shallow graves the
cost to feed a starving generations need to understand the
futile endeavors of man.

Many tears have fallen with more to come. Narrow the
path it is secure, no falling endured. Step by step onward
we go, into the arms of Jesus and our eternal home
with God.

Long the road, hazardous its completion. Sin vicious
and alluring lines the path of a Christians walk.
Righteous the man who evades this madness
called life. Great the reward of a loser in sin.
Place your trust in unseen truths to gather a
promised paradise free from sin.

Madness ensues at the loss of loved ones, unless
seen as a brief pause, a stepping stone to happiness.
What are the benefits of dying a Christian? No eternity
in Hell. What is the comfort to those left behind?
Knowing you are not in Hell

MOONLIGHT OF DEMONS

Music steams the bitter day. Darkness calls its mistress.
Walking dead following the well-worn path. Monkey
see as monkey do in the realm of demonic illusions.
Politicians carry buckets of mud, ready to sling at a
moments truth.

Policemen protect and serve their own interests.
Teachers' teach those willing to learn. The rest are
pushed into the world not knowing how to read or
write.

Demons in the moonlight, darkness the shelter.
Enough light to cause false security, a comforting
prolog before a souls death.

Though possible to hide from man, it is impossible
to hide from God. Humans keep a watchful eye,
they are here, demons in the moonlight,
sin disguised as innocence.

MY WAY

I did it my way
and God watched.

I let sin in my life
and God watched.

At appointed times,
I died and God
watched.

Then to Hell I went
and God watched
as the Angels sang,
there goes a man
that did it his way.

MYSTERY AND LIGHT

Smoke filled life, seasons change, so should we.
If only answers were in questions. If complexities
were revealed as simple.

Then politicians might be honest and truth matter.
What was mystery is now light. What was death is
now life.

Laws sufficed in needed times, but were insufficient
for future needs.

Blood for eternal cleansing, works when applied
correctly.

Freewill received from God cannot replace his direct
commands.

Mysteries and questions abound, a Bible for the
answers. But let the reader beware, plus and
minus is not allowed in Gods world.

NATURE AND ME

Flowing meadows
green and gold,
moss, weeds
   and
morning dew

The rabbits hop,
the crickets chirp.
Snakes rattle
   as
squirrels scurry,
   in an
epic tale
   of
natures life.

NEVER SAY NEVER

With life is hope,
striving always
to understand
what pleases God.

Reading, praying
day in, out, 100%
given to insure a
home in Heaven.

Never, a thing of
fairytales and myth.
Never, a loser's fate.

Never say never a
Christians reality,
a reality of faith
with promise.

I WILL NEVER
SAY NEVER.

NEW BEGINNINGS

New beginnings, loss of innocence,
failed assurance, less is more.
Childhood necessities, grownup
mandates, want versus need.

Time shrinks, clocks ticks, death
nears, eternity calls, judgments
assured.

ONE NIGHT

One night is not forever,
unless tomorrow does not come.
Then eternity becomes reality
and today does not end.

Un-forgiven sins condemn.
Sacrifices were made to give hope.

Life can surprise, but don't let one
night of sin surprise you, with an
eternity in Hell.

PLEASE DON'T FORGET ABOUT ME

I may be old, twisted, immobile,
my ears may not hear too good,
my eyes not see as good as they
use to, but I am still alive, still
here, still feel.

You come to visit, you smile
and say hello, but who are you
speaking to?

Do you see me as a human being,
or just an old person in a nursing
home?

I was once young I had a family,
and I am the reason you exist.

You have a life, I understand,
things to do, places to be, but
please don't forget about me.

RIGHT OR WRONG

Trying to do what's right live
a Godly life, never sure I'm
right.

Desires could be wrong
or right. Attractions of the
senses makes one wonder
if what seems right is wrong?

Gods plan assured and true
Human sin always present,
glittering, tempting, deadly.

Heaven waits, Hell too, will
our efforts be enough to please
God.

SCREAM

Chances given, hopes dashed.
Bloodshed, testaments given
for instruction.

Nothing to come, it's finished.
All is given judgment comes.

Jesus returns with fire and
punishment. Sinners will
scream as Christians rejoice.

SOCIAL TIES

Enchanted,
unremembered
childhood
fantasies.
Adult lies
told to
foster
social ties.

TAKE CARE OF YOU

Child of my creation, grown up, hardheaded but mine.

Mistakes made, sin won.

Sent my only son prove my dedication, but you

hung him on a cross.

Made a home for you, a paradise with me. All I
ask is that you put me first, but you don't.

Other Gods you worship, you sin every day. Seems
you think you don't need me, but still I love you
and if you let me I'll take care of you.

THE DREAM

Dreamt upon our midnight last,
the call of duty to what there
was, as fact and fiction distort,
and our dreams become reality.

THE END OF A LIFE

On a hill called regret, lived a man of no remorse.
He came to be this way, caring for naught but self.

One day in the valley below, a girl called hope,
climbed the hill of regret and met the man of no
remorse.

Was on this day as hope met no remorse, that a
a vision was born. A vision of hope with regret.
and was on this day that new beginnings evolved.

New beginnings of caring for others more than self.
thus the hill of regret became the hill of care and love
for selfishness had died.

You see hope with regret is knowing what can happen
if actions are careless and there is no remorse.

THE PLAN

Where wondrous blessings
once bestowed, became
disaster on a cross.
Gods' righteous plan,
misunderstood, bought
salvation to a sinful
world.

THE PROPHET

A prophet comes,
his perfect blood
to shed in his
fathers war.

A scar upon a
naked city who
knew not God.
A war between sin
and righteousness,
with God winning.

THE THIRD DAY

I am a thief, condemned to die, for crimes I did commit, but this man beside me, no crime has he done. They call him, King of the Jews but they don't believe Jesus is the son of God. He was sent to die for sinners like me and I don't know how I know, but I know he is the son of God.
A mother weeps, a father watches. Tears falling from innocent eyes as life fades.

Jesus I scream, "I am guilty, but you are innocent, remember me when you get back to Heaven." Tears fell from his eyes as he looked at me and said, "This day you will be with me in paradise."

For three hours, the sun was dark as Jesus died. The ground shook, rocks broke, and the temple veil was rent in two from top to bottom.

Three days in a tomb, to rise on the third alive.
Dead, covered in sin, just like the thief dying next to Jesus, but the blood of Jesus, the son of God, gave me life and one day I hope to be able to say thank you.

TO ME ON MY 58ᵀᴴ BIRTHDAY

Happy Thanksgiving
****

Think About It And Prepare
****

If there is no Heaven then there
is no Hell.
But if there is a Heaven, then
there is a Hell.
If there were no Heaven or Hell
then there could be no God.
But there is a Heaven and a Hell,
and there is a God, so think about
it and prepare, for one day you
will face him and be judged.

TRAVELING

Traveling away,
standards delayed,
awaiting returns of
home.

TROUBLE

Did she not know, could she not see?
Those eyes, the deceptive words, but
listen she did, eating forbidden things,
caste out of paradise for sweet, juicy
sin.

Forced into a life of hardship, shame
and guilt, the result of a moments
weakness.

Give the Devil his due, for he knew
what he had done, his punishment just
and sure.

Eves folly wasted on trouble which
could have been prevented if only she'd
known the consequences of pissing God
off.

WANTED

Wanted to fit in, popularity, friends,
ate myself rail thin, until demands
became more then I could do.

I rebelled, was bullied and shunned.
I turned to drugs, alcohol, and sex
to end the pain.

Fleeing from vegetables and health,
I cried a zillion tears, shopped a
million miles.
When nothing solved the problem,
suicide seem the answer, but I
failed that too.
Laying on a hospital bed hooked up
to various machines wondering what
to do, I prayed.
Released with words of stay strong, I
stumbled into church, my last hope.

There I discovered God and learned
I am wanted, and I don't have to
please anyone but God

WHAT YOU NEED

Written on stone tablets, engraved by God,
the words of salvation, but us humans
would not listen. Hardheaded and stiff-
necked, Gods chosen people. Love or
madness, but God would not desert
his people. He sent his son to die for
us, his chosen humanity.

This son dying on a cross, ask his father,
God, to forgive us and he did preparing
us a Heavenly home. all he ask is that we
put him first and obey his commands.

Today with our technology and modern
morals, we are just as hardheaded and
stiff-necked as we have always been.

So after careful consideration, I have
come to realize that what we need is
an eternity in Hell. Then we will no
longer be hardheaded or stiff-necked.

WHERE HAVE YOU BEEN

The Human says:

I looked everywhere searched high and low.
Where have you been all my life? Were you
hiding, do you love me? Do you see me? If
you jumped, I'd scream, if you cried, I'd dry
your tears. Would you do the same for me?

Then God says:

A bolt of lightning flashed the sky, as a
thunderous voice answered, "Child why do
you rant so? "I'm here as I have always been."
"I may not be what you want me to be, I won't
condone your sinful ways, but if you do my will,
I will take care of and love you.

WIDE AWAKE

Sugars coated, sweet and bitter, slick the game.
Greased lightning, fast and friendly, blinded by
desire.

Thought forever seemed a stretch but it broke
before it started. If only awareness had come
before falling dreams hit the rocks.

Mystic visions allure weakened souls. Careless
illusions appeared innocent, destroying hope
and sanity. Mistakes of future regrets did
overwhelm a souls' demise.

Thought a seemingly, complex desire could not
be defeated so I surrendered. It took only a
few months to see that a child could not be
the grownup you need.

It was a fairytale with no happy ending, and
with open eyes I left what never should have
been.

WINDS OF CHANGE

Worship the command, but
appearances deceive. Scared
running away, let down over
all I played. Seemly innocent
glitter beats my resolve at
staying true to my beliefs.

Fought hard, staying straight
the goal. Heaven is the future,
Hell in the past. Certainty not
assured, if the question. Never
stop trying, never give up. One
direction, up the prize.

Final results waiting, winds of
change always present, death
the big reveal.

WORTH IT

What is man's worth,
the sun, the moon?

Where would we be
if not for you?

We are hardheaded,
stubborn and sinful,
but you know we are
worth your love.

Is this not why you
sent your son to die
for us?

I've been everywhere
looking for what was
here all the time.

Now I know what I
forgot, I am worth
it and so are you.

10 YEARS

10 years from retirement, 6 minutes till quitting time, it's almost over a lifetime of service an eternity of??
Preparing for retirement, marriage, college, life on earth, years spent preparing for eternity hoping you
got it right.
The Devil is real, he has prepared a world of sin to trap a soul. Beauty and excitement might thrill the
body but dam the soul. Right now decide, is any sin worth an eternity in Hell?

Poverty runs rampant, the rich snub their noses, the eye of the needle laughs as camels try to pass
through.. Goodness seems a distant memory costing more than most sinners are willing to pay.

Resilience is the key to wading waters of temptation. Blurred lines between sin and righteousness
require a careful study of the Bible.
It may not suit individual desires but Gods commands are final and non-negotiable. Throw up hands,
scream unfair, murmur like an Israelite, but hope the fire of God does not claim your soul.

If the price is right what won't humans do? Well there is a prize waiting for all who are faithful til death and this prize is worth more than all of earths riches, this prize is a home in Heaven, no sickness, no poverty, no death or sin, but it requires putting God first in all things.

A HOLE

There's a hole in the world
tonight.

The son of God just died
and
Jesus was his name.

His blood washed away our sin
and we
did not
seem to notice.

Foretold years ago,
this deaths
cleaning was soon
dirtied up with
SIN.

AN IRISH TALE

Irish eyes so green, potato pie for me,
jig a dance, sing a Celtic hymn.

Dare to fight a war, religious in its
cause.

Pick a side, fair the well my Lady Fae.
Irish gents, make green the color of
my heritage wrapped up in a blarney
skin.

Cascades of rainbow gold a leprechauns
four leaf clover.

Sing of fall, crowns, fairies and queens.
A king of prince his allegiance to the
throne beneath the London stone.

A MILE OF SMILES

Dimpled cheeks, a
mile of smiles.
Marching bands,
circus tents,
spinning rides,
cotton candy
and
candied apples.

It's a child's
break
from harsh
realities.

Tomorrow is
another day,
life resumes,
but today,
dimpled cheeks
a mile of smiles.

A SHADOWS NIGHT

The peaceful calm of a
shadows night.

The restless void of a
days decent.

The unrelenting awareness
of a greater truth.

The knowledge
that life is
no accident
and a higher power
is in charge.

ALL THE HEARTS IN THE WORLD

So long you were not my God. How could I have been so heartless?
It started on a cross. The world watched as the son of God was
crucified for our sins.

The sun darkened the earth shook in 3 hours the world as we knew it
changed forever. Hearts all over the world should have cried, for the
sacrifice Jesus made for us. Oh some did cry, some realized what had
been done.

Blood flowed, death came a burial was done. 3 days later his tomb
was empty, Jesus, the son of God had risen, alive. Then some folks
realized they had killed the son of God.

Unbelievers were heartless, they said, "Jesus was not the son of God."
It did not cause remembrance in them, even though all this had been
foretold in the Old Testament.

What humanity did not understand was that if Jesus had not died for our sins,
we'd have no hope of a home in Heaven.

I have been heartless, but no more. God is my father, his son died for me.
What life I have left will be used trying to be worthy of the sacrifice Jesus
made for me.

ANGELS AMONG US

Life is short, death comes quick,
sacrifice and suffering seems the
norm.

Careless actions fraught with fear,
serendipitous sanctions, frozen in
time.

A wayward mustard seed carelessly
strewn, has now become the whole,
shelter for the lost and lonely, comfort
in the son of God.

As with the faith so sparingly felt, so
shall this tiny seed shine the light of
redemption, for all who would its'
blessings share.

ANGELS IN PLAIN SIGHT

Lonely child on the street corner,
homeless man in a cardboard box.
Lost and ignored, angels in plain
sight waiting for help that never
comes.

Innocent though he was, Jesus
suffered in human hands for
our sin. Humans, created for an
eternity in Heaven, killed the son
of God.

Humanity will face an eternity in
Hell if they don't help all Angels
in plain sight.

"Forbid them not," said the son of
God, "for such is the kingdom of
Heaven."

Will you ignore Angels in plain
sight?

BECAUSE OF LOVE PT.2

Because of love a virgin was chosen
to give birth to the son of GOD, and.
the angels sang this is love.

Because of love GOD watched as his
son was crucified on a cross for our sins,
and the angels sang this is love.

Because of love Virginia and Sasan Lak
were given AUDREY a human angel to
love and raise,
and the angels sang this is love.

This daughter, is God's way of saying its ok
my son died for your sins, because if he
had not died, Audrey would not have a
home waiting for her in Heaven.

Virginia, Sasan, can you hear
the angels are singing this is love.

DAYS

Days of remembrance, names assigned
for to celebrate this or that. Leaves one
wondering trying to figure out what
day is today. Is it necessary to celebrate
any day?

It seems harmless, but these days are
not free. Cards, gifts, food, it's a trick on
someone and I think it's me because I'm
broke and there's always a day needing
celebrating and there don't seem to be
anybody cutting me any slack

Maybe after I'm gone they'll make
my death day a national holiday.
Sure seems fair since I celebrated
everyone else's day when I was alive.

DON'T FORGET ABOUT ME

As a child safe and secure, I thought I had the world figured out.
Go to church, tell the truth, work hard and pray whether things
are good or bad.

Then one day death took you and I did not know what to think
or believe, so I cried. 1 year later I had just accepted that you
were not coming back, when dad married and I got a step-mom.

Dad passed away at 79, Now 4 years later you lie on a nursing
home bed dying and I pray.

A life of 58 years, good and bad. One thing I pray for most
is mom, Dad, -step-mom, please don't forget to remember
me.

Tonight as I pray I know you God have never forgotten to
remember me. To say thank you would never be enough,
but I am so thankful you remember me even when I have
acted like I had forgotten you.

Soon this earthly body will return to dust. Soon the eternity
of my soul will be in your hands. Please don't forget to
remember me.

EVE

You eat because God
created humans.
You drive cars because God
created humans.
You have babies because God
created humans.
All we have to be
thankful for
is because God
created humans.

You get sick because
Eve ate that fruit.
You have pain while
giving birth because
Eve ate that fruit.
and one day
you will die because
Eve ate that fruit.
Don't you
kind of
hate Eve

FLOWERS OF A FUTURE REALM

Flowers of a future realm, steamed in mystery, masked confusion. Breaking news, fuel societies that think they know the truth.

Paper clowns, strings attached to empty promises designed to dull the senses of otherwise clever folks..
Were it not for the few that care, where would we be?
Can it be, this human populace seeks to find what never was lost?
Spending millions searching to find origins that are written in a Bible. When will man's endeavors be realized for what they are, futile?
If it worked there might be reason to continue. Failure is our now, our future in question.
Elections abound results final. Questions fall like the rain of broken glass, a hail storm of doubt and betrayal.
Sharp but sure destinations without God. Sweet and eternal Heavens home, for folks who never stop fighting the Devil.

Imperfect, unable to be perfect, yet Jesus knowing this still died for us.

FOOD SAFETY AND LITTLE DEBBIE

Were would we be without Little Debbie and Uncle Ben Could we survive without
Aunt Jemima?
What about Ben and Jerry's, Campbell's and Swanson's. There would be a whole lot
of whooping
and hollering if people could not get their Eggos.

I remember when you could eat a cantaloupe and not need life insurance, and is there
anything better then home grown tomatoes, unless someone decides to mass produce
and not worry about food safety.

When did America become so addicted to food that it forgot about the thousands
that are starving in the rest of the world? My dad said, "if you get hungry enough
you'll eat anything. "Yesterday a mother who could not get food stamps for her
and her two kids, drove to the local welfare department and shot herself and
the kids. I don't think this is what dad meant.

If life can't exist without worrying about where the next meal comes from and if
this meal is going to kill us, then what does this say about humans. I love my brands
and I eat them and hope they won't kill me, but at least right now I have
food to eat. Seems a little Manna from Heaven is called for. Oh I forgot, God
doesn't do that anymore. Those Israelites didn't appreciate it anyway. They sat
around complaining about it all the time

I guess a Godless world, which we have become, has to fend for itself unless
you are a Christian, then God who knows what you need won't let you starve.

GOD IS HERE ALWAYS

GOD is my friend.
God takes care of me.
GOD I want to shake
your hand and say
thank you.

God you sacrificed
Your only son for my
sins.

GOD I love you and
I love your son.

If I live to be 100, I
can never do enough
to repay the debt I
owe.

Friends come and go,
God is here always.

GOD ON OUR SIDE

Sin runs
blood red,
Doubt
seeps in.

Careless
responsibilities
threaten
a peaceful
existence.

All is lost
if God
is not
on
our side.

GODS' CREATION

On restless nights the moon kissed sky,
its' river of stars swallow in darkness.
A world torn between daylight and
moonlight.

Under Heavens watchful eye Gods'
creation is slowly destroyed as
humanity struggles to be the last man
standing, the last man alive holding the
key of redemption, not accepting a souls'
forever, destined to the black day
reserved for all sinners.

A HIGHER TRUTH

The peaceful calm of
   a shadows night.

The restless void of
   a day's decent.

The unrelenting awareness
   of a greater truth.

The knowledge that life
   is no accident,
      and a
   higher power is in charge.

I AM FREE

A tortured soul, a wounded spirit,
threatens nothing because I am
    FREE.

FREE from doubt, from no hope
   to live life serving God.

FREE to live life as sin free as
        possible.

From a life of no hope,
to a life of hope
and promise,
a Home in Heaven
if I have pleased God.

I am as perfect as any human
     can be, I am
FREE, FREE, FREE,
    and I love it.

I WAS BORN

I was born I die, 2 absolutes I can't escape.
Seems foolish to even fight but I do.
Freewill given, foolishly used.
I'm not dead, but I'm getting there
but I'm getting there.

I've been a sinner, been a Christian,
had my soul walking straight towards
an eternity in Hell.
Now I choose a different path,
a straight and narrow one but
one walking towards Heaven.

The road is rocky and often
I stumble and fall, but
every time I get back up and
keep walking.
I don't know where my walk will
end, but I hope it ends in Heaven

I WAIT AND WATCH

Here I wait. High above the earth,
watching the humanity I created
as they live the life I gave them.

Sometimes I laugh sometimes I
cry, always I love them. If I
could die, my love for them
would kill me.

Life is hope, death judgment.
I am longsuffering but I did
create Hell.

Here I wait come when you
want. I will wait until the end
of time.

IF GOD WAS HUMAN LIKE ME

If God was human like me,
would he live his life as I do?
I am not perfect but I can be
a Christian.
I am a sinner but I can repent,
and all sin.
One day I shall die
and I will be judged,
my verdict revealed
on that day.
As I live my life
a question must be asked.
If God was Human like me,
would he live his life
as I do?

Eternity depends on my answer.

IF I COULD

Faraway the wind did howl,
the moon quaked, the seas
rose.

I in my mighty fortress pace,
scared of the outside world.
Wanting to lose these fears,
not knowing how to begin.

Your independent minded
self-cares for little but you,
as I and my fears love 'til
death.

Faraway God watches as I
try to lead this independent
minded man into your arms.

Here on earth I pray and wait,
this fortress I've locked myself
in shields me from the world
but not the reality that someone
I love could feel God's wrath

IN YOUR ARMS

In your arms was a flame
that promised
to keep me warm,
But
in your arms was hidden
a fire that threatened
to burn my soul.

In Gods arms
was real warmth
that would keep
me warm.

In Gods arms
nothing was hidden.
In Gods arms
my soul rejoiced,
safe and secure.

IT'S MY LIFE

It's my life
to live as I chose.

It's my body
to do with as I please.

It's my mouth
to say whatever I want.

It's my world
and my

Yes, but God
created you
and your world,

so it may be your life
but God
decides your
eternity

LONGSUFFERING UNTIL DEATH

A jealous God watches, longsuffering and just.
Think there is time, the world still exist?
Really, but do you still exist? In life is hope,
possibilities to get it right, but life is fleeting
here one minute gone the next. If you died this
minute where would spend eternity?

God is longsuffering, but life is not, one illness,
an accident and longsuffering ends. Waiting for
the ideal moment to please God, think carefully,
will your life continue until the ideal moment?

Gods longsuffering ends with your death, prepare
now.

MY SOUL'S NOT READY

My soul's not ready for the fire of Hell.
My heart's not ready to hate or feel anger.

My soul's ready for the light of Heaven.
My heart's ready to love and be loved.

What could sin ever offer to keep me from
the ones I love?

What is the purpose of life if not to thank
God for creating you and giving his son
to die for your sin?

What part of obey do you not understand?

NEWBORN RESISTANCE

Frail resistance, jailed intents.
Cautioned care, slayed to rest,
doubts and fears. Warm embrace,
soft response, a protected home.
The cost of being a newborn child.

NOT A DREAM

A palace beyond the stars created
of materials unknown to man.

No suffering, no pain, no loss of
any kind. Sickness vanquished,
death defeated

If only we believed, if only faith
was strong enough to accept the
truth.

Heaven is not a dream, neither is
Hell, and we have a choice where
we spend eternity.

NOT ENOUGH

Guess the blood in my body and the miracles I did wasn't enough.
Should I say forget you and your friends?

Guess being crucified on a cross for your sins wasn't enough.
Should I say forget you and your friends?

You're fair weathered, I'm forever. Your friends deny me, I forgive them.
Should I say forget you and your friends?

Guess a home in Heaven wasn't enough, guess Hell looks inviting, and Satan a
friend?
Should I say forget you and your friends?

Guess the Bible you got wasn't enough, guess my father was right when he said
"he wished he'd never created you."
Should I say forget you and your friends?

You proud arrogant stiff-necked humans why won't you behave?
Oh well, take the freewill you were given and do as you please,
just be sure, you know what you're doing, because if your wrong,
a Hell is waiting and you will burn forever,
while Gods Christian children are in Heaven singing and happy.

You want me to say forget you and your friends?

ONE

One God,
one soul,
one Bible,
one Heaven,
one Hell,
one Devil,
It's all we got.

One Jesus
to die for
our sins,
one Holly Spirit.
One of everything,
but one is
all we need.

UNDER THE RAINFOREST

Winds of a rainforest, the quiet steps of a fairy nymph.
The music of a silver flute played with the fingers of
an elfin man. Twinkle, twinkle, natures' harmony,
gardens of a symphony bathed in a morning dew.

There is a muse, its character flaw to be the one
and only inspiration for a mothers love.

The Fae of a fairy realm hidden from a mortal
world, who long ago ceased to believe. A
fairy world threatened by iron and church,
but saved by tithed bread, lives beneath this
mortal world, not because of necessity, but
for a desire of things un-had in other lands.

With a belief in God for humans yet not
themselves, these Fae exist, hidden but
real, if only in legend.

If these humans only believed and
accepted what lay beneath them,
maybe humans and Fae could
co-exist for the good of all.

RIVER OF SHADOWS

A river of shadows its hollowed sound.
Doubt and fear, bring on the noise. Tis
a waking sea of a beautiful world
scared with memories of once before.

Remembrance does no good but to
keep the past alive. Is death the end or
just the beginnings of past promises
put in motion?

In a country stained with sin can one
more or less of anything repay the
sacrifice Jesus made for us?

If blood washes us clean, can sin wash
anything but the consciousness of
right and wrong?

ROARRRRRRRRRRRRRRR

Think you're bad, the eye of the tiger,
where are your clothes?

Think my rules can be broken?
Who told you that? Not me.

Think my love won't let me hurt YOU?
Who told you that? Not me.

Read your Bible? I hurt the Israelites when they disobeyed me?
Will you ever not be stiff-necked?
For years you used your freewill to do as you please.
My heart aches over some of the things you have chosen to do,
but one day, you will meet the real eye of the tiger
one day you will hear me ROARRRRRRRRRRRRR and it
won't be pretty

SANDS OF TIME

A brisk breeze, a slow wind, scattered
bits of life, blown throughout the
universe.

Born to serve a God, his son risen
from a death suffered for my sins.

Morning comes and goes, twilight
begins its end. The dark of midnight,
its shadow crossing a day at rest.

Sands of time scattered, waiting
for the end, an eternity it can't
predict anymore then can we.

Moment to moment lived of its
fullest in service to a creator so
powerful he can destroy his
creation and one day when the
sands of time have run their
course, in his judgment he will.

SET FIRE TO THE RAIN

Will he not set fire to the rain?
Will he not watch it burn as we
scream his name?

Has there not been given many
chances, did we not see it was
inevitable? He punishes the
Angels who sin, how could we
think to escape his fire, when
we continue to disobey his
commands

If even the rain is not immune
to Gods fire what chance is
there for us unless we do every
thing he commands.

I hate to see the shock these so
called men of God will feel when
God says depart false teachers
I know you not.

SILENT RAVINGS OF REALITIES TRUTH

Fallen leaves of emptiness, a fools request,
a child's detest. The sun of brighter days
caste aside with doubt and fear. Realities
truth, the shattered ruins of consciousness.

It's hard to understand incomplete, silent
justifications, for throwing in the towel, as
is said, for ignorance of the truth.

Ignorance abounds when the blind don't
see the right before their eyes. Ravings
accomplish nothing but to fill the air with
noise.

We've been given a book of answers, so
there is no excuse for not obeying Gods
commands.

SIN AT WORK

I've seen peace, seen war and hate.
I've seen sacrifice, seen the results
of unrighteous, ungodly living. I
saw the son of God hanging on a
cross. I saw the blood of this man
wash away sins. I saw him buried
and 3 days later I saw him risen
and walking alive on the earth.

I've seen love, seen righteous living
and repentance. I've hung my head
and wondered why, could they not
have seen the truth beneath the lies?

I now have hope, given by the blood
of this innocent man, Gods son.
Through Baptism and righteous living
there is a home in Heaven waiting for
me, I just have to get there.

I love you Jesus, thank you for dying
me. One day *I hope to tell you in
person.*

SILENCE

Evening falls on listless souls, their life a hard pressed spot, the technology of the moment. Their God is dead, replaced by video games and you tube clips. Hell is their word for life on earth. Heaven a Disney movie. The victim of reality TV and Hollywood, humans sit and wait for death and taxes, while watching QVC and HSN. Credit card debt is at an all time high while the man who invented it never made a penny off it.

Thin people are called fat, while the fat folks eat a burger and shake at McDonalds. Image is everything, this is why young and old starve themselves to fit into a size 0.

Silence is said golden, then the newsmen start talking and then it's all over. Half-naked men and women grace the covers of most magazines in the racks at the check-out counters, seen by folks of all ages and we wonder why our girls get pregnant outside of marriage.

Our role models have become unmarried stars, pregnant with who knows who's child. Living for the moment, we sing, drink, fornicate, do drugs and whatever makes us happy at the moment. Never worrying about a soul or an eternity which can't be seen because it requires faith. Homosexuality is in God is not.

We wonder why life is hard then we hurt each other for a few minutes of fame. Youth is what matters in this society. Old folks are put in nursing homes and left, seldom visited. Then they die and are buried.

Soon very soon we are going to meet the real King, God, and he won't be silent about his disapproval with how we have lived our life. So surrender to his will or burn.

STORMS OF DOUBT

Opportunity to forgive and forget, in hands
I scared by damage done in drunken states.
In weakest moments life and death decisions
rest in charity given by the most unwilling.

True regret fades into freedoms web of
hurt and fear.

Shelter or redemption let God decide as
storms of doubt blown away by sweet
revenge, save the life of a damaged
child safe in a cellar.

SWEET TO RISE, LEFT TO CHANGE

Lock and key slammed and touched.
Fostered in old and rent, scarred
remiss, desire the culprit, less is
more.

Deemed assured, skills missing
needed for survival. Change
comes ready or not.

Readiness avails itself in times
of need but is unheeded when
things are good.

THE ALL SEEING EYE WATCHING

Driving to my destination,
the sky covered in clouds,
blue and white mixed in
such a way, giving the
day an artful color that
brought joy to my trip.

As I watched the colorful
sky a thought occurred.,
hey, God is up there
there watching me and
I smiled.

THE ART OF SIN

A glass of wine,
cherry red lips,
their volcanic
glow.

In the dark of
midnight, the
intensity of fire,
a sinners desire.
The art of sin.

THE BIRTH OF A SOUL

In a small Podunk town, the child of a mother
grew up.

This child attended Bethel University and fell
in love..

Years later a marriage was held at this Bethel
University.

This child now teaches the children of the
future.

Soon she will have her own child to teach,
a human angel, with a soul.

This child, created in love, a human angel
with a soul, will be a blessing.

This child, a human angel with a soul has
now arrived, the cycle begins again.

THE FEELING

All along there was a feeling, this hole in my soul,
I was sinful, stubborn and unbelieving.

Then one day, light from Heaven shined into my
dark and God said, "come closer."

Round and round we went, 'til I threw up my
hands and said, "what do you want God?"
He said," look how you live your life, you are
broken and I died on a cross to save you."

In tears I came closer and was handed a
Bible and ask to read. I read and prayed to
understand.

I begged for forgiveness. I didn't know exactly how I felt,
but I needed saving, so I was baptized.

I screamed, "Jesus, God please stay, I need you." Then
God smiled and wrapped his loving arms around me
and I slept.

THE UNENDING HEART

How big is the human heart?
How big is the world?
How much does God love us?
UNCONDITIONALLY.

From the smallest infant
to the oldest man,
the heart loves.

Life is pain and suffering,
life is joy and happiness
too.
If the human heart
loved only friends and family,
what a small world it would be.

How big is the human heart?
   Unending
      Unending
         Unending
            Unending
               Unending

THROWN OUT WITH THE BATHWATER

A baby makes its' way thrown
out with the bathwater.

Loosened to free battered and
bruised, weathered through
storm.

Jesus its' light, Heaven its'
goal, Hell the defeat, sacrifice
the journey, resistance its' key
to victory in death.

WHAT A MESS

It started as a paradise, but a piece of fruit started
a mess that has grown to epic proportions, lying,
stealing, killing, all manner of sin, and when the
going gets tough we blame the government, God,
anything and everyone but our self.

In the Old Testament times the Israelites made a
mess, they were pooping on the ground and not
covering it up, so God told them he was unhappy
about this and for them to cover up their poop.
They immediately covered their poop up.

That was then now we have freewill, but God still
does not like it when we make messes, he just
doesn't say anything directly to us like he did
to the Israelites.
See freewill allows us to make all the messes we
want to, but do not think for a minute that just
because God does not reprimand us directly he
is not going to on judgment day.
So don't be like that man that hid his talent, or the
7 foolish virgins. Keep a watchful eye, clean up
your messes and when the shit hits the fan you
will come out smelling like a rose.

WHATEVER IT IS

Life happens, death comes, judgments too.
Whatever it is there's no use in crying.
Whatever it is I must go on.

Sitting, feeling lost and overwhelmed.
Seems like someone is watching me
through a 2 sided mirror.

"What do you want from me?" I ask.
I don't know how to surrender, I
don't know how to give up.

Whatever it is, bring it on, I will put
one foot in front of the other one until I
can't no more, then into your hands
I will put my soul.

I know it's you God watching me through
the 2 sided mirror. I know it was you that
gave me my soul, and I know you know
my heart, so I know you will do my soul
right.

WHERE ON THE WATER

Weather unpredictable but sure, cares to show its face, winter, fall and spring. Summers heat melting frozen cares. Wayward though it seems, possible where there ends, waters wetness flown on waves, human in its glory.

Startled bits of proof, traveled miles of consciousness, ignorant of its truth. Where within is jarred, traces, guilt accountable only to itself. When on water flown life, is peace found, fears allayed, 'til time is spent and eternity come.

Knowledge known faultless, hastens to enslave. God and man, indifferent to the wishes of either, cling to an illusion of control, which does not exist.

God rules, but will not make his creation do his will. Though he sent his only son to die for our sins, we refuse to live life without sin. Humans think they have control, believing they can do whatever they want, not not accepting that the freewill they use is a gift from God.

One day it ends as was destined from its creation, when Eve ate the forbidden fruit and sin entered the world. Then it will be seen, where on the water we have been and where on the water we will be, when the water is gone.

WHERE WITHIN

Where within this
sinful world lies
truth and
righteousness.

There within
resides complete
destruction
thrust upon a
humanity that
refuses to
accept Gods
authority.

WHERE YOU BEEN

Where you been all my life?
Sin came and went. I fought.
Lost some won some,
trembled at the sound of
your voice.

The Bible was my comfort,
my shelter from the storm,
but in my deepest despair I
wondered where were you
God?

It was at the point of death,
I realized what I had known
all along, you had always
been here.

So should you ask where were
you? Remember, I am here
where I have always been.
Where you been?

WILD SINNER COME HOME

Hasten to receive, truth and knowledge.
Never think you are too wide for the
straight and narrow.

Many follow the crowd hoping for
a magical happenstance that never
comes.

Glitter and promises of Heaven on
earth sway the wild sinner, but do not
fulfill anything.

Come home wild sinner run if you can,
walk if you can't, but come home before
the Devil claims your Soul.

A CHRISTMAS LIE

Trick or Treat, air or meat.
Nickel and dime the
dollar died penny too.
Plastic rules, credit sunk,
who cares?

Santa never was Tooth
Fairy either. All lies we
tell our children then
expect them not to lie to
us.

A JIVE OF CHANGE

Are you ever going to change? You never you never seem to.
Are you still some loser, baby? You still got your sin, new
clothes, different hair style, more makeup, same you.
Jump off the train, slide down the street, you still a rose
full of thorns.

Gangster love, black widow, how you amaze me. Such
foolishness, rain of fire, heat's a coming, strike. a pose,
down you go, Hell for sure,

Unless..........

What do you know about Jesus? Do you care? Have
you heard you should seek knowledge, find the
answers. There's a gate to enter, lessons to learn,
service to do.

What are you waiting for the gate won't open unless
you do what God wants. Enter at the risk of salvation,
enter at the risk of killing the Devils hold on you, enter
if you want a home in Heaven, but enter or burn in Hell.

A LIFE GONE WRONG

Silent quietness
of
a whispers voice.

Invisible warmth
of
a summers day.

A chilling wetness
of
a winters frost.

The bitter thoughts
of
a broken heart,
its
shattered remains
of
a life gone wrong.

A MOTHERS' ROSE

As the dark descended
thoughts flooded, the
beauty, the innocence
of your soul.
Red for love streaks of
white for purity.

A mothers' rose made
from a world that knew
not sacrifice or putting
others before self. This
was your life.

The light that filled my
soul is gone but its' memories
last and so do you in everything
I do.
A mothers' rose is all that's left
to remind but nothing made
can ever replace mother.

A SANTA STORY

Santa's gained a few pounds,
decided to Jenny Craig it this
year. Weight Watchers he tried
Atkins too, neither worked. If
only he could resist all those
cookies left for him every
Christmas.

Oh well, if Jenny Craig fails
Mrs. Clause will just make his
suit a little bigger and Rudolph
and the others will just have to
work out more.
I'm sure carrying all his weight
must be hard and chimneys
don't get any bigger.

But don't worry children if you
don't have a chimney he'll just
come in a door.

A SOUL WITHOUT A HOME

Yes you are a soul without a home,
but be prepared, because a soul
covered in sin can't come in my
home.

My son died for your soul, covered
its' sin in red blood, so if your soul
is not still stained red don't bother
knocking on my door.

Hell is the home for you. The Devil
doesn't care what color your soul is
as long as it's not red.

Just scream and come on in. Hey, you're
going to be screaming once inside, might as
well start now.

A TINY TALE UNIMPORTANCE, MAYBE

Loose lips sink ships, a stitch in time saves nine or something like that, but Americans love a whistle blower unless it's them getting whistled on, and who sews these days? Not me or most folks. We go to Wal-Mart and hope someone's made some clothes that are decent for anyone over the age of fifty. The younger sect wants to show as much skin as can legally be done. A few old codgers have followed suit, but that's just wrong, disgusting even. What child wants to see their mama or grandma half naked? It used to be wisdom came with age, not face book and you tube. These days' social media substitutes for friendship. If Harry met Sally today it would be via a dating site, and as for the scene where Sally pretended to fake an orgasm, what's the point with Adam and Eve selling sex toys online.

Cows jumping over the moon are so yesterday, now they sell chicken for Chick-fil-A. Guess the man in the moon, oh yeah there is no man in the moon. If there ever had been, the first moon walk would have scared him off. Three blind mice should have known better then to chase anyone. Now De-Con wants what's left of them to come to supper. Foolish Mary too contrary raised twelve kids in a shoe because she refused to buy a house.

Injury lawyers are a dime a dozen, no payment unless they win. Guess things don't mean what they use to. I remember when hot anything meant it was hot, but not anymore unless you really don't want to get burned, either that or you want a lawyer to sue whoever made the hot thing.

Knock offs are all the rage now. Basically it's getting a shirt that looks like a hundred dollars for twenty.

Then there's road rage, well what can be said if you give an idiot a car and a gun? Just hope you can drive and have life insurance.

We've come a long way baby, indeed, Bell South has been joined by Verizon, Sprint and other cell phone providers. Now you can talk to anyone anywhere while driving and if you can't talk you can always text. I believe such behavior is called distracted driving, right up there with drunk driving only worse because even your grandma can talk and drive. It's no wonder grandma got run over by a reindeer, Santa most likely was texting the North Pole while driving. If you think the world is a crazy place and it could not get any worse, well think again. Looks like a woman is running for president and she just might win. If she does win, well God ain't exactly been too froggey friendly with us women ever since Eve ate that fruit.

AMAZING YOU

Spinning, blowing, flowing, soaring
amazing incredible you.

Created in Gods image, loved and
cared for you.

A home in Heaven waits for you.
Are you coming? Step lively, walk
the narrow road.

There's a Hell down below, don't
go there.

BORN LOST

A frightened child sits in a corner
wearing yesterday's clothes,
covered in last nights' supper.

Anger rules in a house that bans God.
Abuse, neglect and death paint the
walls of what should be called home.
Safety never existed here.

Crawl to the door runaway if only the
strength will come.

No milk carton will picture my face,
because no one will miss me. I was
born lost.

BRAIN RAMBLINGS

Yeah that's it, here there they flow. Thoughts, idle nothings probably, but something needs to change. The world sure is a mess. Maybe some brain ramblings might just do the trick. Either that or we wait for God to fix it.

He did create it he knows just how to fix it. Oh right some of you don't believe that.

Well the Devils counting on that. He was bad from the start. That's why God sent him and his friends to Hell, where he waits for us. Us meaning the sinful among us. The righteous get to go to Heaven. Are you righteous or sinful? Do you know?

BROKE TOE TUFF TOE

Broken toe? Shattered calm,
steep concern. Wading
waters of decision, to
treat or wait.

Time moves slowly as tensions
mount their attack.

Doctors, sharks in the water.
Money, money, give or stay
home. No dollar no see.
Guess walking will wait

Broke toe tuff toe
never know toe.

BROKEN

The broken ones,
bitter angels.
broken
by a
broken world

bitter at the thought
that the humans
they guard could
one day
be destroyed
by a
jealous God.

CHILDHOOD ENDS

Childhood ends
where I begin,
a living soul
accountable
to God.

Teen years
confuse,
warranting
careful
consideration.

God
understands
but still
expects
obedience

CHRISTMAS 2013

Soft grass wet from dew.
The moon full and silent.
A night wind blows.

Owls hoot, crickets chirp.
Children asleep wait for
morning light to see what
Santa has left under the
tree.

DEEPLY ODD, ASSUREDLY STRANGE

Guess imbecile suits me fine.
I am deeply odd, assuredly
strange.
Rebellion not, surrendered
and muted of course.
Hey listen up, what do you
want from
an autistic poet with MS?

That's not enough?
Well kiss my grits.
Bye, I hate grits.
Ok so I save a few lives,
not.
Eat Jello, Eggos and applesauce,
Woo woo breakfast is served.
I'm still deeply odd, assuredly
strange

ENTER THE ODDS

Enter the odds, chance rules.
Luck of the draw,
winner take all, Losers are
the majority.

The children are crying.
There's no money for
food.

Their milk and cheese buys
lots of chances to Rich Ville

Much money will buy lots of
food.

IF ONLY I WIN.

ENTER THE WOLF

To seem alone
in a world of
beauty and
wonder.

Enter sin masked
as harmless fun.

When I felt alone
the wolf came
and I was no
longer alone.

Now he's gone
and I am alone
again, only this
time God is
gone too.

FAITH

Can you feel it?
Do you see it?
Of course not,
that's why
they call it faith.

Will you feel it?
Will you see it?
Sure if you end
up in Hell

FALLING NIGHT

Midnight is falling, daylight locked up in a moonlit night.
Followed the world found sin.

Followed God found Heaven. There's no comparison,
burn or sing.

You did not choose to be born but here you are. Hell
might not be where you want to spend eternity, but
it is where you will go if God is unhappy with you

Don't look for Heaven in any human. You were born
and one day you will die. Your eternity starts at death.

Seems foolish to let a falling night end with you
unrepentant.

If you are hoping for another day, one more
chance, I pray you get it because if you don't
and God decides to end this world,
ohhhhhhhhhhhhhhhhhhh.

FEEBLE MATE

Carry on my feeble mate,
rest assured your time is short, lest
you ache for what matters least.

The prize reserved is worth more
then anything imagined could ever be.
Clocks tick, chimes ring in a new year
With its challenges of sin.
Temptations take on a new glow, alluring
yet deadly.

When there seems not anything left to think up,
well here it comes
When will it end?
When the one who created it
destroys it.

FLESH AND BONES

Flesh and bones,
a soul that can't die,
all you, all Gods.

Flesh rots, bones break,
and disintegrate,
blood flows,
Spirits vanish,
God waits
judgments come

FOOLISHNESS 1,2,3

Deadly Fun
Riding, partying, and acting stupid.
Up down, across a thousand miles.
Now is all you got.

War:
We dig graves, such a waste, when
death is so final.
Must we kill so quickly, so unnecessarily,
when a moment's hesitation could
Make all the difference.

The End:
We behave so careless sometimes
how do we hope to
escape eternal punishment

GIBBERISH OF THOUGHT

Sharp and square
forward pass.
Jump aside
up a tree.
Down below
In a hole
out beside
lain away.
Through it all
look to learn
new beginnings
doomed to end
far too soon

GOOD NEWS

Good news, you don't have to burn.
That's right, fire won't come near
you if you listen to God and put
him first.

Yes and stop whining about that blood.
Maybe you didn't ask Jesus to die for
you, but thank goodness he did or
you'd have no hope.

HEALTHCARE WOOS

Can't afford to be sick
but sick I am.

Can't afford healthcare
but can't afford not to
have it.

Too poor to live, not
time to die.
God, you handle this.

HOW LONG

And God said:
How long will I need you?
How long will I love you?

And man said:
How long will I love you?
How long will I need you?

but God said:
You have not loved me.
You have not thought you needed me.

The answer came:
How long will I love you,?
How long will I need you?
Is forever long enough?

I WILL NOT GO QUIETLY INTO THAT NIGHT

You may think you can do what you choose
and you can, but don't ever think I won't raise
Hell if my needs are not met.

Freewill is every bodies mine included and if
I fall because I trip over your cat or something
else you have left in my walkway, I am going
to fuss and maybe not politely.

You want to be treated like the old folks at
nursing home, then act like them.

I have no power to change anyone but myself,
but when I can't even take care of me, I will
not go gently into that night

IF YOU THINK

If you think
Hell can't hold
you, remember
God created the
earth and put
you here and
it's holding you
pretty good.

IS THERE ROOM IN GODS HOME

As the wind rises its sadness weeps.
Lightening sails across a night sky.
Happiness screams as puddles of
melted snow seep down a
mountain side.

Drops of broken tears clutter the
silence of an impending realization
that all will be destroyed.

A life lived has ended, its soul waits
to be judged, will there be any room
in Gods home for it.

IT IS NOT

It is not in man to direct his own steps.
Look around you, death and destruction
everywhere.

I saw the weather reports, snow and cold
everywhere, even places where it is not
the norm

A man froze to death in his car when it got
stuck in the snow.

Will man ever accept that nothing can
change unless we accept that God is
running the show.

LATE

Lateness can evolve into cracks in an otherwise solid soul.

Late for school, for work, you are late for everything. You
wear lateness like a second skin.

As the world spins around the sun you spin through life.
There is never a chance of moss clinging to you.

Slow down or not, there are two times you will not be
late, your death and your judgment.

LIVE UNTIL YOU DIE

I have MS yes. I have balance issue which cause me to fall, so I use a wheelchair when I am out of the house. People think it strange me using a wheelchair when I can walk, but I can't fall as long as I am in the chair, so let them think me strange. The balance is just one of many issues MS gives me but yet I am still here, still alive, so I refuse to give up. What is the point of giving up? Ok one day I will die as will we all, but until that day happens I am going to do whatever I can. My kids don't understand how I can feel good at 11:00 then drive somewhere in the sun and feel like crap at 4:00 and several hours afterwards.

There was a song that said live until you die and what else can anybody do. Wish your life away, sing too, it won't do any good, you're here until you're not. I thought long and hard about my MS. I said to myself, self, is it anymore right for someone else to have MS then it is you? Let's face it, what kind of person would want anyone else to have MS? Definitely not the type of person I would want to be.

God watches his children which I am proud to be one of and he wants me not to give up so I don't intend to. Every day I go to a nursing home to visit the 100 or so friends I have made there and believe me when I say there are far worse things that could happen to me besides MS.

Every day, I see folks that in whatever shape life has put them in, are living the best way they can. These friends of mine have embraced their lives and live. Yes often some of them die and I grieve, but never do I regret the time I have spent being their friend. What happens after their death is Gods decision, but while they were alive, I did whatever I could to make them happy.

One day God will see me on judgment day and it is my hope and prayer that he is pleased with the life I lived while alive. If he is I will get a home in Heaven where no one will have MS.

This is my life with MS, and I will live until I die. My happiness does not depend on not having MS, it depends on God.

MERRY CHRISTMAS DARLING

All year long you've put up with me,
my quirks and general f--- ups. Now
it's Christmas a time to give, to say
how much you mean to me.

There'll be no Kay Jewelers under
any tree or anywhere else in the
house, but love will be everywhere
because I love you that much.

Merry Christmas darling.

MUSING FROM THE BARSTOOL

Searching outside our self for answers locked inside. Seeking absolution in a bottle. The Garden of
of Eden calls us home, but our ego bars the way, and our friends are idiot winds offering shelter
from their storm. Our dreams are fairytales, yet we dream of another life. Sleepless nights, Little Boy Blue in the corner. We stuck our thumb in the pie and all we got was fat.

Serving fear and anger, security drowns in paranoid bondage. **Desire is endless, attachment the price. The reality of illusion is trapped in a subconscious s maze. Driven by ravings of** f blind men we align ourselves with the walking dead.

We sit in a room of last hope and yellow brick roads, evading the problems of our world. Sober thoughts from drunken minds, what foolishness. The truth sits on a barstool witnessing it all. A silent testament to guide us on our journey to freedom. Why won't t we surrender to the process of existence? We have no control.

Let's start a spiritual revolution, the asleep must wake up. The false gods will get angry but we must burn the fairytale books. The contracts have been signed, soldiers hired to sell us more dreams, feed us sleeping pills to stop our wake up call. More drugs sex, chains, the king needs slaves, it's the false gods decree.

All the while the aware ones scream, get up fight the lies, and end the separation from the only God. Wake up humanity before it's too late. Sit down and shut up, silence gives you freedom to study the Bible and know what God wants you to do.

ODE TO A CHICKEN

Peck, peck, like a typewriter.
Corn to eat, water to drink.
Cluck, cluck sing your song.
Walk your chicken walk.

Sorry to say but one day
someone will wring your
neck and you'll end up
cooked on someone's
plate, hopefully mine.

I love you chicken, my
stomach too, thanks for
tasting so good.

PEACEFUL BEINGS

Peaceful beings they seemed
until God sent his son, then
cold bloodied murders they
became.

On a hill hanging on a cross,
dripping blood to wash away
the sins of humanity, hung the
son of God.

These callous humans did not
understand what they had just done,
but God did and when his son ask
him to forgive them he did.

POEM FOR A FROG

Green you are
jumper too.

If flies were gold
you'd be the richest
frog ever.

PREPARATION

Clarify the world to me
make it clear for all to see.
Stamp out poverty, stop all wars.
Desire to worship the only God there is.
Throw out the red carpet, he's coming
back to end it all.

Lace up those shoes, zip the zippers.
Lock the life once lived, so it does
not become a stumbling block.

Treasure Gods greatest gift,
the life of his son,
for without it life would
just be a preparation for
Hell.

RAIN

Her name was Rain.
I had a chat with Rain today
Customer support you know

Windows sucks, Bill Gates too.
Had to buy a new computer
Problems galore for a tech
idiot.

Where was my 30 days' notice?
Even renters get 30 Days before they are evicted.

Rain fixed the problems until there are more,
Tech idiot I am.

Do I live to compute or is it the reverse,
whatever, Rain is the bomb and
I am the idiot.

Thanks are not enough, but thanks is all
I have to give, new computer took
all the money.

REPRESSED DESIRE

Swallowed up in a sea of lies,
to awake at the sound of the
thunder of an impending storm.
The rain of careless living for
a moments pleasure.

The carnage of desire
unleashed from repressed
bodies threaten a soul.

Souls scream for they
have become entertainment
for the rich.

Arise behold the light of fire
Jesus comes, it ends now.

RICHES

Riches and Fame are the Devils tools.
He didn't buy your soul he already
owns it.

Keep trying to get that camel through
the eye of the needle. Hope you succeed
before you die.

Oh there will be some rich folks in
in Heaven but will it be you?

If you doubt me read the Bible its
all in there.

RIGHT CAN'T BE WRONG

You can't make right wrong,
you can't make wrong right.
Legalize it, worship it, doesn't
change a thing. Wrong is sin
and it will always be sin and
God said he will punish all
sinners and he don't lie.

SEE JOY

See Joy walk, see joy fall,
see Joy blow her whistle.
See help come. See ching,
ching,

Nothing is faster than the
speed of light except
money and it comes and
goes so fast, you never
really see it but you know
it's there by the stack of bill
on the coffee table.

SELLING YOUR SOUL

Can you sell what you never owned?
I guess you could try.
Wouldn't work though.
God calls the shots
he made your soul and
he will give it
to the Devil if
you piss him off.

So if you ever hear
anybody say they have
sold their soul to the Devil,
you tell them
It can't be done for
he gets it for free on
judgment day
if you are a sinner.

SITTING HERE AT LAST HOPE

Here I sit sick and scared, not knowing what to do.
sure I'll make the wrong decision. I cry to no avail,
pity parties don't really help anyway.

Just when I almost threw up my hands, I prayed.
I said," God please take over I'm not doing so
good on my own."

In a moment, calm came where before had
been fear and insecurity. The tears stopped.

Life will end as will all life, but God will be
at the end just as he has been since the
beginning.

When things overwhelm I must remember I need
someone stronger than me
I NEED GOD.

THE BIBLE

Do what you want with my Bible.
Doesn't matter how you got it.
I gave it to you. It's the only book
I wrote. Read it don't read it, burn
it, throw it in the garbage, it's your
choice, your freewill, but remember,
one day you will die, then you will
stand before me and be judged for
how you used my Bible.

THE BROKEN ONE

Thought I had it all, Batman and Superman
rolled up in one boy, then mama broke her
leg and daddy got drunk and I realized my
two hands were not enough to do it all.

I cried, prayed and begged daddy not to
drink. He just hit me and drank some
more. Mammas leg, healed, my heart did
not.

Here I sit grown up but broken. Daddy
drank himself to death. Mamma cried
until there were no more tears to cry
then she died.

What is my life? Am I no more than a
then a broken one, a shattered human
Incapable of healing.

THE CHILD AND THE ANGELS

Late one night when Christmas had come,
the cookies eaten, the milk drank and the
presents opened.

Late one night, a child was heard to say
thank you God for everything, then she died.

Years of pain and suffering were now over.
No more wondering why life had to be so
hard. No more of anything.

Her parents wept as the angels rejoiced
and took her home.

THE DAY BEFORE

The day before life went on, I sat by your bed and held your hand. You looked at me with knowing eyes. You couldn't speak, but I believe you knew I was there. I thought I saw you smile twice. I must have told you 100 times I loved you. I would have kissed you but these crazy quirks of mine would not let me.

Around 4 pm. it was soon to be time for my medicine, which I had left at home. I ask the nurse if I had time to go home and get it. She said," I can't promise you anything, she could live 3 more minutes or 3 days, but you must take care of you." I told mom I had to leave and go get my medicine. I could tell by the look in her eyes that she did not want me to go. I left after telling her I would be back as soon as possible.

It took me an hour because I did not live in the city where she was. I prayed the whole time I was gone. I said God please her live until I get back. When I returned she was still alive, I said mamma I'm back and I won't leave again. I put my hand on her bed and prayed thank you God. 5 minutes later she breathed her last breath.

I thought what am I going to do with my life now? See for the past 5+ years I had been at the nursing home every day to take care of mom. Now she was gone. I walked to the door of her room and looked down the hall. There outside the door were all the friends I had made in the 5+ years I had been coming to the nursing home. Then it dawned on me, my life did have a purpose, a whole nursing home full of people whom I love and who love me. I am full of sadness but I will always remember the day before my life went on.

THE FINAL COUNTDOWN

Paint to color a universe
Stripped of all its beauty.
God creates, man destroys

Time slides past a future
It knows not when will
come, but it will come
at Gods choosing,
the final countdown.
Will I be ready?

THE NEW RED CAR

How many hits on the head does it take to pay for a new red car?

Where was the love in all that anger?
When did I love you drown in a bottle at the corner bar?

How many nights did I sleep in fear hoping you would not come
in my bedroom and wake me up?

The new car drives great but the memories of abuse make the
ride rough.

How many hits on my head, I did not count, but when I turned 16 I
left home to drown my anger at the corner bar.
I am now an alcoholic

THE SPEED OF DARK

Fast as a soul can scream, darkness descends,
cluttered with sin and desire.

Evening never came but with its tempters
snare.

Push it away, light the candle, flip the
switch.

Mirrored personalities, right and wrong are
blurred in this gray sea of life.

Tempting though it seems, the image of
an innocent man hanging on a cross for
my sins clears the mind of a soul surrounded
by darkness.

Fast as it was, its speed unknown, darkness
shatters at the scream of a soul bent on
Heaven.

THE STORM

Lights dim, wind trashes a night sky, as drums of thunder roar.
These are the songs of a universe. The melodies of atmosphere
surrounding a world created by God.

Dance to my ladies fair, nature wants to exercise. Silent water
floods as rivers rise. Trees topple, houses made wet. Children
splash in its splendor. Creations symphony plays to a full
house

Tensions mount as peace is disrupted. Could this be the end?
Electric surges, damage everywhere, safety in question.
Sirens sound the threat pray and seek shelter.

THE STORY OF MY LIFE

I ran from myself but got caught by me.
The story of my life is filled with sin
and redemption. Desires fulfilled
damaged my soul. Sin avoided changed
my future.

I was headed down the wide road to
Hell, I met many people on this road,
not one worth an eternity in Hell.

The teachings of my youth led me back
to the narrow road leading to Heaven. I
have not met many people on this road
but the ones I have met are good
Christian people.

My life's story is unfinished, its end
comes at my death. It is a story filled
with ups and downs and I hope God
will be pleased with how it ends.

It hasn't been easy to live a Christian life
in a sin filled world but I think I got the
end of my story right. I hope you agree God.

THERE IS BUT ONE

Formed by the vastness of the whole, a God flawless yet
angry at a people created and chosen by him, a people
who choose to worship gods made by their own hands
instead of him.

'I am God 'he said, 'I know of no other. There was no
God before me and there will be no other God
ever."

How can man begin to think that any god made
with his own hands can do anything for him?

Humans worship many things and act as if they
are magical something which can help solve
their problems.

It might be a lottery ticket, a rabbits foot, a
tarot card, anything but God.

There is but one GOD, no matter what you
believe one day you will believe in God.

TO BE CONTINUED

From dust I came, to dust I return.

My life exists because God
wanted it so.

Where or when it ends I
know not, but my life is
unfinished.

A million thanks would
never be enough,

I am a work in progress,
to be continued.

TO WEEP

I am a sinner
trapped
in an earthly shell.

A Heavenly father
watches and waits
for my
repentance.

As days
pass and time flows,
on bended knees
I pray and weep.

WAKE THE SLEEPERS

Wake the sleepers' mister sleep,
childhood ends where you
begin.

Stock the soul mister box boy.
Send the invoice check the inventory.
Less is more the IRS says. More
beneficial to us that is.

Wake the sleepers, the wedding's started,
the door is closed and you've no key.
Didn't they say, were you not told?
Trim the wicks fill with oil. Guess you
thought you knew best, seems you were
wrong.

Funny how some folks think they can
sleep it all away. Shame it is not that
way because then we might all get into
Heaven.

WASTED LIFE

Talents are wasted on a broken soul.
Nothing ventured nothing gained.
The security of a million fears.

Gated communities guard what
never should have been. Mixed
reactions to issues of trust.

Pipe dreams fuel a sense of well
being, as fake as the sleep that
created them.

Rainbows of promise were for
floods not fire. Fire is promised
to all hard hearted humans.

Technology can create anything
but salvation or forgiveness.

In the end when all has been
said and done, will our life
be a tragedy or a love story.

WHAT'S IN A NAME

What's in a name?
Everything if that name is Jesus.
What's in a name?
Everything if that name is God.
What's in a name?
Go to Hell and find out.

WHO, WHAT, WHEN, WHERE

Who am I? What is my purpose?
When is it finished? Where will I
spend eternity?

I am Gods child.
My purpose is to serve him.
It is finished at my death.
Where I spend eternity is
Gods judgment
based on how I have lived
my life.

Souls are judged finished or not.
Who, What When, Where,
GOD.

WEAK AND OLD

Weak and old
I lie on a hospital bed
waiting for the medicines that can
save my life.
Old and cold,
my life in the hands
of the doctors.
Have I forgotten that just one drop
of the blood of Jesus
is all it would take to save me.

TO GAIN THE WHOLE WORLD

He shelled out miles of redemption
You chose immeasurable punishments.
Tried and true out the door. Bird in
the hand now KFC.

Soiled soul clean or die. Registered
attempts at salvation useless unless
followed through.

To gain the whole of everything means
nothing if on Judgment Day God sends
you to Hell.

TELEPHONE RING

Ring Telephone Ring,
catch a drift, wade a
storm. Lease a life
not your own. Poor
but proud the cause
of your damnation.

SLEEP MY CHILD

Sleep my child morning comes too soon.
Wake the stars uncover the moon, darkness
falls sunshine sleeps.

Sleep my child all is at rest. The wind so
softly blows its calming release. The day
is locked in night.

Sleep my Child, dry those tears, for God
is watches over you.

SHE SAYS SHE'LL KNOW GOD

I ask if the baby could go to Church with me.
She said, "no."

I said, "How is she ever going to know God."

She said," Oh she'll know God."

How I thought how," He doesn't live in your house."

Then it dawned on me the doors might be locked
but the phone is not. A long distance phone call
will be my way to get God in that house.
This child will not go to Hell
if I can help it.

This Child will know God

MY NONSENSE

A Diller a Dollar, a 12:00 scholar
who was dumb before 12:00
and will be dumb again at 1:00.

Clip Clap hoofs on the roof.
Reindeer taking a rest while
Santa scots his booty down the
chimney.

Caught a falling star burned a
hole in my new jeans. Guess a wish
would have been better.

Lost in the mirage of life, Lights
burn their sinful glow luring the
weak and unsaved among us.

The Devil laughs as God cries.
Lambs to the slaughter we have
become.

MOMENTS OF MADNESS

Colors explode, painted on canvas,
drawn on paper, inked on cards
artistic expressions in moments of
creative madness.

Words explode typed on computers,
written in diaries, on paper or cards
poetic expressions in moments of
verbal madness.

Desires repressed can lead to sinful
behavior acted out in moments of
physical madness.

Moments come and go, a minds
madness brief or eternal depends
in its righteousness

LOST

Born an innocent blue eyed infant, safe in the arms of love,
living an idyllic child's life. Tonka trucks and Barbie, cookies
and candy, fun and games was life for me.

Church and school was my weekly routine, it was all I knew.
My family told me "I needed to wake up or life would pass
me by." At church I sang, prayed and learned Gods will.
I thought "Wake me up when I am older and wise."
"Wake me up when it's all over." Then one day I was
older and wise. I woke up and knew I was lost
Obedience and Baptism came next for me. Childhood
had been a preparation for righteousness.

I don't know where this journey will end but I
know where it started and I know where I want
it to end and what I need to do to have any hope
of getting there.

HEAVENS PLAN

Written in the awareness
of an infallible being.
carried out by servants
adopted into Heavens
plan.

Existence before creation,
fulfilled in its own time.
Repeals fruitless, but
punishments are assured.
with disobedience.
Rewards are guaranteed with
obedience.

Knowing which comes in
Heavens plan.

GET OUT OF MY WAY

Don't block the door I'm coming through.
Stand aside Mister Sin. Shoe box all those
temptations. Save them for, SAVE, no not
that. Burn them, throw them in the trash.

No the Devil does not want them, that's
why you got them. He's got plenty remember?
Did Jesus die for some all upping temptation?
No, no, no.
He died for you and your sins.
Thought you were clean? Well you weren't.

No I don't know what burning flesh smells
like, but it can't hurt like burning you.
Red not your color bet you won't like fire then.
But you can't have one without the other

Your best thing is to do whatever God has
said and avoid all this Hell and fire.

ANTICIPATED CONFUSION

Vast expanse
sullen degree
littered release
scared intent.
Doubt the most
savor the least
restrictive of all
a world of OZ.
Fantasy at best
animation for sure.
Reality at risk
sanity in question.
Coming and going
running away.
Torn in pieces.
Thrown this
moment.
Last is first
well is all.

ABSURDITY

It was a flip flop she lived in, what use to be was not now. Up was down, in was out. Confusion the norm, and political correctness ruled.

"Give me a phone show me a number, let me speak to a real person," she screamed. "Has keep simple gone out with Obamacare." Congress can't seem to agree on anything it seems, except Americans are their pawns, and this is an easy way to make a living.

As she pondered on this, she realized, she couldn't afford to live or die." The electric company not care, "pay the bill or read in the dark, "they would say. The water company would care either. Money, money, is the real game the days.

Life has become a game today, the poor have lost before their first turn, the rich cheat, hell invented the game, and the middle class folks go to jail, don't pass go don't collect 200.00, it's monopoly for real. Boardwalk is lined with pimps and hookers selling escapism money, drug dealers have set up pharmacies and doctors have been replaced by nurse practitioners and physicians assistants.

She got a call today, a man said he wanted to sell her some burial insurance, when she told him she, had already bought her funeral, he said there were always incidentals that it wouldn't pay for. She thought, "I'll be dead let the kids pay for the incidentals." He said someone would call later about a policy to cover the incidentals. She said, Goodbye," and thought," what an absurdity."

She remembered when Bob Dylan had written a song about having God on our side, now he does interviews where he says he has sold his soul to the devil. What the crap is that?

There are some people that say God is dead in America, as if he could die. She shuttered at that but she could see why it might seem that way considering how some humans act, but God is just as alive today as he has always been. He loves us so much that he sent his son Jesus to die on a cross for our sins. All this because we would not change our sinful behavior. One day though, God is going to say I have had enough of these sinful humans and then we will change. I know some folks will like it but some won't "Oh well," she thought "You pays your money you takes your chance." "If the price is right, she thought, we'll be dancing with the stars in Heaven, if we have guessed wrong we will be dancing in the flames of Hell."

She knew America had outlawed prayer in school, forbidden the creation theory to be taught, but allowed the Big Band and Evolution theory. "Seriously, she screamed, we have traded God for a monkey, a spoken word for a loud noise and 7 days for millions of years." I guess we forgot that God rested on the seventh day and he looked at what he had created and said it is good." Humans, if they work, work 7 days so they can pay their credit card debt and plat the lottery. She doubted God would approve but humans don't seem to care what God thinks about how they live their lives.

In America medical bills are pushed aside in hopes of good health, then we die and the funeral homes refuse to bury us on credit. We are then cremated our ashes sprinkled nowhere, because no one cares about us. Nursing homes house the unwanted; the few wanted folks spend all their money to live there, not even having enough left to be buried. She could only imagine what happened to the unwanted nursing home residents when they died.

It's a hard world we live in, but live here until we die we must. There is a paradise promised us in Heaven, it's in the Bible, but in order to live there we must obey Gods commands in the Bible. Few choose to do this using the freewill they were given to do as they please, then fussing when things don't turn out as they want them to. She wondered, "Why anybody wouldn't want to live in a place like Heaven?"

"Doesn't it seem silly she thought, to spend your whole life trying to be healthy, then dying anyway?" See it's a time thing, die today, die tomorrow, but one day you will die. Then Evolution ends because you have evolved into a pile of dust, unless there is a God and he did give you a soul. Then you will sing or scream depending on how you used the free will God gave you. "Let's face it she said out loud, we humans are screwed, we got little money and little hope of anything changing. "We fuss about what ever president we have at the moment, then elect another one to fuss about 4 years later. It's a government of I can't fix it but neither can you so let's just fuss about it and maybe no one will notice the mess they are in. She doesn't care much for TV but How I Met Your Mother is a popular show where a gay man tries to convince the audience he is a woman chaser. It must work because the show is a big hit. She had always loved men but where had it gotten her? Poor and penniless. "Maybe she thought it would have been better if she had been born gay. At least she could eat and pay bills."

Twerking is all the rage and she does not even know what that is except if you are Miley Cyrus and you Twerk a married man on national TV, you get richer and your picture gets put in all the popular magazines. "Wow who knew, she thought, all these years I have worked in factories for minimum wage and now I am disabled and can barely afford to eat. I guess I should have been Twerking instead." Whatever happened to the Bible verse that says if a man don't work he doesn't eat? I doubt Twerking could be considered working and always remember MS. Cyrus made her money because her fans attended her concerts and bought her CDs and merchandise.

She had thought Clueless was just a movie until she tried to get Obamacare. Now she is afraid the one thing she thought was supposed to help her is so complicated that by the time she gets it, she won't need it. Remember she has bought her funeral and she will get Medicare sometime in 2014 unless they pass another healthcare law that does away with Medicare.

"Gods' plan is so much simpler, she thought just obey his commands, die and go to Heaven where there is no Twerking and no Obamacare.

"Woo by the looks of things, I might need Heaven soon, she shouted."

ABOUT THE AUTHOR

Joy Olree is a poet and she paints with toothpicks. She is married with three children and eight grandchildren. She has Asperger's Syndrome and Multiple Sclerosis. She is a Christian.